DARK BLUE SUIT

DARK BLUE SUIT

and Other Stories

PETER BACHO

University of Washington Press

Seattle and London

Copyright © 1997 by the University of Washington Press
Printed in the United States of America

Library of Congress Cataloging-in-Publication Data
Bacho, Peter.
    Dark blue suit and other stories / Peter Bacho.
      p. cm.
    Contents: Dark blue suit—Rico—The second room—August
1968—Home—A life well lived—The wedding—A Manong's
heart—Stephie—A matter of faith—Dancer—A family gathering
      ISBN 0–295–97664–0 (alk. paper). —
      ISBN 0–295–97637–3 (pbk. : alk. paper)
      1. Filipino Americans—Washington (State)—Seattle—fiction.
2. Migrant workers—Washington (State)—Seattle—fiction.
3. Seattle (Wash.)—Social life and customs—Fiction.
4. Filipinos—Washington (State)—Seattle—Fiction. I. Title
II. Title: Dark blue suit
PS3552.A2573D3   1997   97–24806
813'.54—dc21   CIP

The paper used in this publication meets the minimum requirements
of American National Standard for Information Sciences—Permanence
of Paper for Printed Library Materials, ANSI Z39.48–1984. ∞

To Vince, Rico, and Vic
who, seventy years ago,
sailed from Cebu to Seattle,
the new home they would never leave.

Contents

DARK BLUE SUIT

Dark Blue Suit

First there were the men, Filipino men. And though they came
from different Philippine islands, when they got here, they called
themselves *Pinoys*. Most were front-line immigrants, but not newcomers, not for years now. Some had come in the 1930s, many
even earlier. As young men—little more than boys, really—they'd
left their homes, pushed out by poverty and pulled to this land
by adventure and the promise of a new start. And through the
years they'd told a wanderer's unchanging lie—yes, we'll be
back—to thousands of parents and lovers, sisters and brothers.
Most never went back, and you can find their bones in every
West Coast town from Juneau, Alaska, to El Centro, California.

Forty years ago, in the 1950s, they filled the Victory Bath-
house and other low-rent venues, their numbers spilling onto
King Street, the heart of Seattle's Chinatown. At the Victory, a
joint famous among Pinoys, a patron could clean himself in a
private bath, or clean out his wallet at the green felt card tables
in the rear.

They were *Alaskeros*, men who went each spring to the salmon
canneries of Alaska and returned each fall. "Sal-mon season,"
they called it, sounding the "l."

Seattle was their assembly point, the headquarters of their
Union, a militant and powerful one that dispatched its members
to the canneries. Filipino immigrants, many just out of their teens,
built the Union in the 1930s; it was a source of pride, not just for

them but for all Pinoys.

For more than twenty years, the Union had faced down racism and the hostility of the canning industry and had survived its own destructive cycles of criminal control and purgative reform. But in the 1950s, it took on a foe more dogged and dangerous than its own tendency to implode. The federal government, prodded by Senator Joe McCarthy, was taking dead aim at the Union, recently reformed by a dedicated core of left-wing labor leaders.

The government missed and the Union made it through the decade, dying years later but in its own time. That time came without drama or government interference, with the slow, quiet footfalls of seasons passing. The Alaskeros, who built the Union and founded a Community, are gone now, leaving King Street and the rest of Chinatown to the care of others. But forty years ago Chinatown was much different, particularly King Street, particularly in the spring. . . .

From places as different as San Francisco and Walla Walla they came to Seattle, just as they had for twenty or more earlier springs, laying down their dishrags and field knives—the tools of dead-end jobs—for a chance to go north and make Union scale. It also meant a chance to see old friends who, at season's end, vanished with pockets full of cash and mental lists of places to spend it. Or to see once more the pristine Alaskan landscape, a universe removed from hot-plate rooms in Frisco or the dust of Eastern Washington fields. Not everyone went—there were always more workers than work, greater supply than demand—but everyone hoped, at least every spring.

From a distance I can see them still . . . then closer, as my father and I approached. Despite their poverty, most dressed well, wearing suits that Filipino writer Carlos Bulosan called "magnificent." Their splendid clothes and, more impressively, the easy sense of elegance with which they wore them, stood out against the drab backdrop of cheap hotels, pool halls, card rooms, and the dull apparel of Chinatown's year-round residents.

That day, like most days, Dad was also wearing a suit. This one, though, was especially sharp—a somber, dark blue suit, pressed and perfect, fit for a mayor, a movie star, or an Alaskero. "Like Bogart," I heard him mumble earlier as we left the house for Chinatown. "Got to look good," he said. "Show the boys."

At almost five years old, I didn't know much about my father. He didn't talk much, at least not to me. Maybe it was the language. Mine was native English—fluid, made in America. His was borrowed and broken, a chore just to speak; Dad preferred Cebuano. The English I did hear from him I imagined he saved, hoarding words that twisted his tongue. To me, they came mostly in the form of monosyllabic blasts, barked commands to "do dis, Buddy . . . now." And of course, "dis" got done—now, never later.

A man of mystery, my dad. I did know that every summer he would leave us for three months to work in a salmon cannery, only to reappear every September, loaded with money and a level of generosity that would disappear by the end of the month. Other than that, I knew little about him. On the ride over, I decided to find out more.

"Dad, what are you?"

"Wha' you mean?" he replied without looking at me.

"What's your job in Alaska?"

"Foreman."

"Dad, what's a . . ."

"Big shot," he said, and laughed.

"Dad . . ."

"We're here," he said, as he pulled the car into an empty space. "Come on. We got three blocks to go, and I'm gonna see my crew."

We walked briskly to our destination, lower King Street near the train depot, where hundreds of Filipino men, maybe more, were gathered. For two blocks they crowded both sides of the street like a holiday and leaned against women, mostly white. Well dressed and taller than their male companions, the women looked genuinely pleased that the Pinoys had picked this spot.

I recognized two of them—a tall, pretty blonde and a tiny redhead—from other trips to Chinatown with my folks. One day Mom, Dad, and I were walking in one direction while the redhead was going the other way. Just as we passed, she glanced at my father and smiled a quick little upturned twitch. Mom didn't notice, but Dad did. And just as he did with me, he looked straight ahead. At the time I wondered how a person so small could smell like a garden.

But it was the men who mattered, at least to me. From a block away I heard their voices, and as we approached, the noise grew louder. Through the din, I could make out some words, English words, and I heard songs and long peals of laughter to stories or jokes spoken in languages we didn't speak at home.

I'd been to Chinatown many times before, but I'd never seen it this way. Chinatown had somehow shed its drabness to become an outdoor cabaret, with samba the music of choice even without a band.

We paused at the edge of the crowd while Dad carefully straightened his hat, a flawless Borsalino of finely woven white straw. He turned to look at me and must have sensed my apprehension.

"Don' be scared," he said, and grabbed my hand. "I'll tell you who's good and who's not."

His strong grip erased my fear. It said I was Vince's boy, which, even then, I knew wasn't a bad thing to be.

"Psst!" someone hissed nearby as we cut through the crowd. My father didn't turn to look, but I did.

"Psst!" There it was again. I traced it to the old hotel two doors up from the Victory. A stylishly dressed Filipino—I didn't know him—was standing in the doorway. He started walking toward us, fast.

My father turned to see who it was. Dad's face showed faint recognition but no sign of warmth. Then, as the man kept coming, Dad shot him the Look. I knew the Look, having had it recently applied to me at the dinner table when I balked at having to eat my mother's latest fare, boiled chicken over rice with a side of pork and beans. I ate it, but only after my mother's pleas had failed and she'd invoked my father to employ the Look.

As I stood there, I was pleased at having my father's stern gaze directed elsewhere. I knew it worked on me but I wanted to find out if it had universal application. I didn't have to wait long.

"Hello, Johnny," Dad said. His tone was flat, almost lifeless, and his greeting, if it could be called that, came from between clenched teeth and lips that didn't move. As he spoke, he released my hand, folded his arms across his chest, and created a barrier that said *stay back.*

Johnny pretended not to notice. "Vince! Vince!" he said enthusiastically. Real or feigned, I couldn't tell. "Jus' got in. Long time no see."

"Yeah," my father replied. "Long time."

"Me and you, " Johnny said. "I go with you this year."

Dad said nothing.

Johnny, sensing a wall and hoping to avoid it, swerved sharply and turned his attention to me. "Good-lookin' boy," he said, with a smile that I knew took great effort to maintain. "Wasn' here las' time I was up. Big for four."

"Almost five," I corrected him.

Johnny bent low toward me. He was so close I could see small beads of sweat on the round tip of his nose. He reached into his pocket and pulled out a handful of one-dollar bills.

"For candy, Sonny," he said as he pushed the loot toward me.

I didn't like this man much—he was pushing too hard— and I knew Dad didn't like him at all. I'd never before taken money from someone I knew I disliked. Nonetheless, my judgment was blinded by the vision of scores of Hershey Bars, purchased by the box; I wasn't sure how many, but I knew it would be more than I was then able to count. The candy was as good as mine— I could already see several boxes stashed safely under my bed— but only if I moved before caution stayed my hand.

"Thank you," I said as I shot my right out, quicker than a jab, palm extended, fingers curled like talons about to close.

For Filipino children of my age and generation, it was almost an instinctive reaction. Bachelor "uncles," friends of my parents, old Pinoys with no wives or kids, doted on us like we were their own, and for a few days each spring and fall, we were. But of course, we weren't, which meant that we, the recipients, were always on our best behavior, as were they, our transient bene-factors.

"Ah, Vince, you really dunnit," they'd say after visiting our too-humble frame house. Their wistful tone said they could have "dunnit" too, given a break here or there, and that maybe they still would. But then again, after twenty years in the new land, maybe not.

Filipino American kids and our legion of bachelor uncles—a case of old gold-toothed smiles meeting young gap-toothed ones. They gave us gifts and small wads of greenbacks plus stacked columns of coins, and, like public television, we accepted donations gladly.

But I knew that this welcome tradition might not be honored because of my father's ill-concealed dislike for Johnny, my newest potential donor. I figured I'd just close my eyes, grit my teeth, and grab the cash, all in a smooth, circular motion that would end with the money in my pocket—a deal hopefully done before Dad could say *Don't take money from jerks like Johnny.* Speed was the key, but this time I didn't have enough.

"No," said the voice, stopping my hawklike swoop just short of its target. I didn't have to look to know I was too slow, or to know that Dad's audio had a visual that could clot my blood. Defeated, my hand fluttered then fell, a useless, guilty appendage that hid in my front pants pocket. I wished my pocket could hide the rest of me.

I summoned the nerve to look at Dad, not directly—I wasn't that brave and kept my view to the ground—but rather through a darting series of eye movements, from the centers of both sockets to their peripheries and back. These visual contortions provided safety but also produced a headache, forcing my return to center focus—I'd seen, though, that the Look was focused not on me, but on Johnny, my discouraged patron.

"Ah, Vince," I heard Johnny say in a whiney voice that could have been mine. "It's jus' money." I knew then that Dad's gaze frightened everyone, not just me.

"No money," my father said. There was no whine in his voice. "At least not from you."

"Ah, Vince," Johnny pleaded. "I . . ." he said, and paused. "Never mind," he said softly. "Never mind."

I knew without looking that Johnny was moving away, retreating beyond the range of Dad's evil stare. I felt a tug on my arm and instinctively followed my father.

"Come on," he said.

We continued our walk along King Street. I looked back and saw Johnny. He'd resumed his post in front of the old hotel, staring after us dejectedly. To my quick look, he shrugged a reply. Neither of us knew what he'd done to earn my father's wrath.

"Dad," I asked meekly, "how come you don't like him?"

"Thief," he said, then paused, as if "thief" were just the first of a full deck of bad names. This confused me; my father had friends, close ones, who were hard men. Some were thieves; others, even worse.

"Thief!" he said again, in lieu of an explanation. I didn't expect further elaboration and was surprised when it came. "Card shark," he added. Confusion again. Uncle Pete was a card shark and also my father's good friend. There had to be more.

"Johnny work with Leo five years ago," my father explained after we'd walked a few more steps. "Not my cannery, I wasn' there. He take advantage on Leo. Almost three months' hard work, Leo come back. Broke. No, worse than broke. He borrow money from the boys but can't pay back. Of course they're mad. I give him money when he get to Seattle. Tell him to pay them and go home."

My father then looked at me. He stared until I turned toward him. "If you not here," he said evenly, "I make that Johnny bleed." I was amazed that his dull monotone could carry violent, angry words so far, so powerfully. Dad could've been at a service station, using the same voice to order "four bucks regular, check the oil."

"Just remember, Buddy," he continued. "You got family, you got friends—back home in Cebu, but 'specially here, where you got nothin'."

My uncle Leo was my father's youngest cousin. I recognized the name and remembered the face, but mostly from photos. He lived in Stockton, and the last time he was in Seattle was the year after I was born. My father felt close to Leo, like a protective older brother. "Leo's good, " he said. "Family. Nothin' better."

By listening to snips of conversation when my parents and their friends talked, I was able to paint a picture of this man who, by blood, had earned a drop from my father's small pool of affection. I liked to think about Uncle Leo, and I longed to meet him. He seemed so childlike, so unthreatening and, unlike my father, so wholly incapable of paralyzing me with the Look. And, despite his age—only four years younger than Dad—he seemed more a childhood comrade than an uncle. A fan of Hershey Bars? I could imagine that, just as I could imagine offering him a bar from my private reserve.

Family legend said that my father and Leo had sailed together from the Philippines, but only after Dad had promised Leo's mom—Leo was only sixteen then—that he'd take care of him. Dad was the strong one, and he'd tried his best, but there were some events even he couldn't control.

"We come this land," Dad's favorite Leo story began, "an' he's sick mos' the way. We get off the boat—Leo's white like a white man—and I says, 'Leo, don' be sick.' He says, 'Can' help it, brod.' We pass two cops on King Street, and he suka, you know, mess all over the street. They take him away. Public drunk. I try to explain, but they don' listen. 'Welcome to America,' they say."

We continued to walk slowly along King Street, Dad pausing every few steps to greet old friends and others he knew and to tell everyone who could hear him that he had his crew.

"Got a slot, Vince?" an older man asked. He shifted from side to side, nervous. I felt sorry for him.

"Sorry," Dad said in his usual monotone. We didn't even break stride.

Another, a slender young boy, approached my father. "*Manong*, sir," he said politely. "Can I . . ."

My father shook his head no, cutting off the boy. "Crew's full; got the last one yesterday." Same brush-off, same monotone. The boy silently stepped aside, but Dad, for a moment, studied him, and his face, always so stern, seemed to soften. "Don' give up," he told the boy. "Somethin' breaks; guys don' show. Stick around; still early."

He then turned to me. "Come on," he said.

His reaction to the boy surprised me. "Dad," I said. "Why'd you do that?"

"What?"

"Be nice to that boy."

"You mean I'm not nice?"

"No, I don't mean . . ."

"What you mean?"

That sudden hard edge. I heard it. Real or fake? Like always, I couldn't tell. Although my father spoke English badly, he did it well enough to make me stammer. "That boy," I said weakly. "That boy . . ."

"Oh," he laughed. "That boy." He paused a moment, then spoke. "Tha's Leo and me," he said quietly. "We come this land and need work. We look like him, full of hope, and tha's all. Lose that after while, too." He stopped walking, turned to me, and gently took my shoulders in both hands. "Tha's all," he said, looking into my upturned face. "Mebbe you understand sometime, but not now. Too young." Then he steered me sharply forward again, tugging my left hand. "Come on," he said, in his brusque monotone. "Gotta go."

"Where?"

"Find Leo. Called yesterday. Goin' with me to Alaska. He's here."

"Where?"

"There." Dad pointed to the Publix Lunch, an old restaurant across the street. The news thrilled me. The Leo of legend, a beacon of kindness and generosity! Family, I thought. Nothin' better.

I walked quickly, matching each of my father's steps with two or three of my own. My right hand, ingloriously felled by my father's aversion to Johnny, had remained in my pocket, afraid to come out. But inside its warm cotton cave, I could feel a rustling.

The hawk, I knew, would soon fly again.

The Publix Lunch was a loud, smoky place on the edge of Chinatown where Pinoys ate burgers on white bread. We entered through the front door, or tried to, at the same time that a burly young white man, a sailor, was trying to leave. "Watch y'self," the sailor snarled as he bumped Dad.

"Go to hell," Dad snarled back without even looking.

The sailor spun around in the doorway—no small feat given his girth—and turned toward my father. Dad shooed me to the counter, then turned toward his foe.

"What choo say?" The sailor's slur came from too much whiskey. I knew. Some of my uncles were drunks.

"I says go to hell."

The place was jammed with Filipinos waiting for dispatch to the canneries. I sat between two of them at the bar—I didn't know either one—most likely from California. They looked at the sailor, now the sole object of attention from all the Pinoys. The man on my left—a dark, pock-marked Ilocano—put his right hand in his jacket pocket. He didn't move. The one on my right also held still, except to breathe deep and long.

Sailor's move. He studied Dad, then scanned the room searching for allies he'd never find, at least not there, not during dispatch.

I'd seen Dad fight, knew his temper and skill, the signs of coming violence, like the slight tilt of his stocky body toward his target (the better to strike first). His short, powerful punches never stopped until his target was on the floor. His leaning stance said there were split seconds till launch, maybe less. Dad would win; he was too quick, too mean. And winning, he always said, was better than losing; especially here, he said, in this land that gave losers no breaks. He and his friends were like that, as were the two men on my flanks, who silently waited, coiled and still, for the party to start.

I couldn't figure it. Dad was a good man, gentle (for the most part), and generous to Mom, my baby brother, and me. But I'd

also seen his anger, vented sometimes at other Pinoys, sometimes at offending strangers like this soon-to-be-sad sailor. His
aptitude for violence frightened me. I didn't want to see this, its
latest manifestation. Fortunately I wasn't alone.

The sailor fidgeted before taking one small step back, the
first move toward a full retreat. Popeye he wasn't. But even if he
was, he was smart enough to guess that Dad was even money in
a fistfight. My father watched him go, then he turned toward me.
"Come on," he said. "Leo's down there."

At last!

"There" was a booth at the far end of the aisle. I could barely
see its outline in the dim light, my vision fogged by smoke from
the grill and from long Cuban cigars and short American cigarettes, no filters. As we neared our destination, I immediately
recognized Uncle Leo from the pictures at home of him and Dad.
He was younger than my father, but traces of gray touched his
hair, while Dad's was still black-coffee black.

He didn't see us approach. He was busy, buried in the chest
of a white woman, the tiny redhead who smelled like flowers. I
wondered why he didn't sneeze. She was holding his hand. Uncle
Leo raised his head to stick his tongue into her right ear. I didn't
understand his goal or purpose. The redhead, however, started
to giggle, her laughter building quickly.

To me, it looked like an advanced, adult form of torture, like
a tickle that goes on a bit too long. I'd have to try it out on Allan,
my harmless and chubby next-door neighbor, the next time we
wrestled and I pinned him to the ground.

I reached the table first; Dad was a few booths back, chatting with friends. Uncle Leo sat next to the aisle, just inches
from where I stood. He didn't notice me, so focused was he on

the redhead's ear. I shifted my weight from one foot to another, uncertain whether to interrupt him. Fortunately, I'd inhaled enough smoke by then; it made me sneeze.

The redhead smiled at me. "Honey," she said to Leo. "We've got company." Leo, tongue still extended, didn't stir.

"'Scuse me," I said.

"It's Vince's boy," she said.

Bingo! Password "Vince." Uncle Leo turned quickly to look at me.

"Sonamabits!" he said excitedly, tongue now withdrawn. "Buddy? Your Dad and me . . . I'm Uncle Leo!"

He reached to grab me, laughing and hugging so hard I was immobile, vulnerable, scared. I thought of his tongue. Having conquered one ear, would it soon nail another? "Uncle Leo," I croaked. "No licking, okay?"

"Oh Buddy, don't worry," the redhead laughed. "He was just saying hello to me. It's something adults do, isn't it, sweetheart."

"Oh," Uncle Leo said, and released me. He seemed embarrassed that I'd seen something adults do.

"Leo." I recognized Dad's voice and felt him brush by me. Uncle Leo rose to greet him.

"Still lookin' good, Manong," Uncle Leo said with a smile. Although Leo was only a bit younger than Dad, he used the deferential term of address usually reserved for men much older.

"Too long, Leo," Dad said softly. Gently, he touched his cousin's shoulder with his right hand, allowing it to linger for a second before letting it fall.

"Good to see you, Vince," the redhead said.

"Hello, Mildred," he replied. Dad gazed at her for a second before turning his attention to Uncle Leo. I was surprised; his look said he knew her, maybe even well.

Dad moved into the booth, choosing a spot on the bench opposite Uncle Leo. "Guess you met Buddy," he said casually. Both smiled. I just nodded.

"Buddy's got company, too," Mildred added. "Here comes my Stephie." She pointed to a young girl who was walking toward us from the bathroom. "Stephie," Mildred said when she reached our table. "This is your uncle Vince, and this is Buddy."

Mildred proudly informed us that Stephie had a recital later that afternoon. "Her teacher says she has real talent."

Stephie was a *mestiza*—even then I could tell—white features and light brown skin. She was older, by maybe two years or so. I was surprised I'd never seen her before. Seattle's Filipino community was small; my folks knew all the adults, and I knew, or thought I did, all their kids.

"Sit next to Buddy," Mildred told her. "He won't bite." She smiled. "At least not like his daddy."

To me, at almost five, the thought of biting Stephie seemed silly (although much less so years later). I giggled, then glanced at my father, who was glaring at Mildred. Typical Vince. No sense of humor.

Dad looked at Uncle Leo, who just shrugged. Then Dad gave a sign—right hand close to his breast followed by a quick flick of his index finger, at himself, then at Uncle Leo, then back again. When he did that at home with my mother, it meant "just between us," a Cebuano conversation, with me excluded.

On those occasions, I'd fake preoccupation with something, maybe the family pet or a new toy, and just listen. I figured my folks thought I couldn't understand, but by coupling familiar words with different inflections, I was able to follow most of what was said. Since neither pet nor toy was available here, I improvised.

"Uh, Stephie . . ."

"It's Stephanie," she interrupted primly.

"Huh?"

"Stephanie," she repeated. "That's my name."

"Uh, okay," I said with a shrug and pointed to a large black case under the table. "What's that?"

"It's my accordion," she said. "I take lessons."

Oh, no. Another one. At every community gathering, after the speeches and before the dance, scores of Filipino kids would gather on a stage, formal or makeshift, and pull and push these boxes of musical terror, coaxing forth variations on "Lady of Spain."

For young Pinoys of the 1950s, accordions were the instrument of their parents' choice. I first became aware of this match (Pinoys and accordions) on a muggy summer night at one of those overlong community functions. The young musicians were pulling and pushing away, oblivious to time, heat, or the pain inflicted.

Dad, all frown and perspiration, had a theory for our suffering. He turned to a neighbor, another victim. "Goddam Welk," I heard him say. The neighbor seemed to understand, nodding at the reference to the accordion-playing band leader. Television was then in its infancy, and "accordioncy" (Dad's term) was in its undeserved prime. I don't know about other cities, but Seattle must have been the accordion center of America, at least for Filipinos.

Welk's popularity spawned a host of imitators among the sons and daughters of poor immigrants and triggered dreams of success (and maybe a national show) for their American-born kids. Besides, accordions were cheaper than pianos. Dad understood this but wasn't sympathetic. "Monkey see," he snorted, "monkey do." His hatred of the music spared me from lessons.

Now you, poor Stephanie. That old devil Welk had claimed another soul.

Stephanie was still talking, but I didn't hear much— something about auditioning for the Mouseketeers, and that Mildred claimed Annette was really an adult with two kids. I was concentrating on the conversation between Dad and Uncle Leo as Stephanie rambled on. Still, she seemed nice enough and more than eager to talk. I just followed her lips. When they stopped, I jump-started the words.

"Um," I said, and beat back a sneeze. That was enough to start another round. She had a bottomless sack of informational gems, mostly about herself.

"My mom says I'm gonna be on TV," she said smartly. "But even if I'm not, I've got a future. I'm half white, you know."

"Oh," I said pleasantly. Your mom's white, I thought. So what? She makes me sneeze. Besides, most of my Pinoy friends are half-breeds of some sort. No big deal. As Stephanie droned on, I nodded to be polite, but I didn't hear another word.

Besides, Dad and Uncle Leo raised more interesting topics, like Mildred's telling Leo that Stephie was really his and that, at the least, he should start paying support (including accordion lessons). Dad just laughed. He said that given Mildred's, ahem, record with Pinoys, Stephie could be anybody's, including his. Heh, heh.

Stephanie my sister? Hot gossip, but I kept my cover by looking at Stephanie and nodding. Dad's comment didn't shock me. I knew that my line of siblings didn't end with my younger brother. There were others—older half-breed stepshadows in faded photographs—whom my parents took great pains not to discuss, at least not with me. (There would be one I'd be allowed to know— only one, and only for a while.) It was a mystery, but not espe- cially pressing. Whatever Dad's past, I was happy at home. And at almost five, that was all that mattered.

Cebuano, unlike some languages, has a nice melodious tone. A harsh message delivered by men—like *puta*, used in refer- ence to Mildred—could be tonally disguised and made to sound so sweet. Fuck the puta, my father said sweetly.

Poor Mildred. So old, so dumb. Years and years with Pinoys, and she still hadn't a clue to Cebuano, not even the frequently uttered puta. Even I knew that one, gleaned from my mother, who said it often enough. She told me on one occasion that it meant Dad's old girlfriends, all of whom had smelly boxes.

Being shut out of the conversation inspired in Mildred a se- ries of facial expressions. At first she was indifferent, then stu- dious, checking her manicure for signs of imperfection. Finally, when the language of exclusion showed no signs of change, she pouted. She rested her sad face atop her palms and extended her elbows toward the middle of the table.

Dad picked up the hint. "Pardon, Mildred," he said in En- glish. "Sometimes we forget. It's jus' that Leo and me get so comfortable talkin' of, you know, back home in Cebu. Plus, we talk about goin' to Alaska—it's been a while since Leo's been there—tha's all."

"Tha's right, honey," said Uncle Leo, building the lie. He duplicated Dad's smooth, sincere tone. Their story seemed to placate Mildred, as did a promise to conduct the rest of their conversation in English. I was disappointed. The best stuff passed

in Cebuano; I felt the door to my father's world—his real one—
closing.

"So, what about Alaska?" Mildred asked. "I hear there's problems."

Dad rocked backed and stared at the ceiling before leaning
forward; he stared at Mildred. Another sign. This one said: Important. Listen close.

"Like I was sayin' to Leo . . ."

A lie, once started, has its own life. Dad and Uncle Leo hadn't
discussed Alaska, but my father was good, persuasive. We all
turned toward him.

"There's problems," he said. "Not for me—got my citizen-
ship years ago—but for guys like Leo. Government's mad at us."

I was confused. "Uh, Dad, who's 'us'?"

"The Union," he explained with a touch of irritation. He glared
at me to make sure I understood.

"Oh."

Satisfied, he continued. "The government says the Union's
Communist. But that's a lie."

Communist. What did it mean? My only clue—whenever I'd
heard the word spoken, even by my father, it was in quiet, almost timid tones. All Filipinos, all Communists, all part of the
Union, or so the government said. I'd even met a Communist
(my mom had told me so) at the Union's last Christmas party.
(The irony of a Commie Christmas party had, of course, escaped
me.) After the kids sang carols, accompanied by accordions (natu-
rally), Dad had introduced me to Santa.

Santa was the Union president, Chris Mensalvas, a brown
little man who smelled like wine and walked slowly with a limp.

As Santa, he was unconvincing; he was out of uniform, choosing to wear just a red stocking cap. Still, I liked him. He was comfortable with kids, maybe even had some of his own. We chatted about television shows and other topics I can no longer recall. What remains is the interest he showed—genuine, I felt sure—and the absence of an adult instinct to ban chatty me to the company of other children.

Even the adults, especially the men, regarded Chris fondly and with obvious admiration. They approached him to shake his hand, conveying best and heartfelt holiday wishes to him (his health) and their Union (its survival).

Later that evening, after the party's end, my parents, my brother, and I were walking to our car. I was curious about Chris and had a list of questions for my father.

"Dad, is Manong Chris a Communist?"

"Jus' never mind," he said.

"Leo," Dad said slowly, "I don' know wha' to say. Thank God, I'm a citizen, but I know you're not. Here's the catch. Lotsa boys in the Union aren't citizens even though they been here long time. Government say when they leave for Alaska and try to return, they'll keep 'em out."

Uncle Leo was puzzled. "Why, Vince? We done nothin' this country. We don' hurt it . . ."

"It's Chris and the other officers. Government say they're Communist. We get rid of 'em, they get off our back."

"So, let's get . . ."

"Don' say that!" Dad said sharply. "They're good men, strong for the Union. Besides, who's nex' we do that? You? Me?" He pounded the table for emphasis, then scanned our small booth for signs of dissent. None. We were all cowed by my father's outburst—even Stephanie, who finally stopped talking.

"Next time, Vince," Mildred said nervously, "just ignore me. Just keep talking in Cebuano, okay?"

But it was Uncle Leo who had provoked the tirade, and upon his own blood my dad fixed his coldest, fiercest glare. Uncle Leo wilted, staring at the the table and conceding the point. "You're right, Manong," he mumbled in a tone full of deference.

Point won, Dad switched again, choosing soft, soothing words to rebuild their bond. "Ah, Leo," Dad began. "Not your fault. You been away." Uncle Leo smiled, glad for readmission to his cousin's good graces.

Balance restored, Dad paused. "I don' know how to say this," he began slowly, "but this season'll be hard. Maybe the government keep you out. Maybe not. You wanna go, I take you. The contract's real good this year, make plenty money."

Dad smiled, then added in Cebuano: "Enough to pay for accordion lessons."

Uncle Leo started giggling, but stopped when Mildred stared at him. "Joke only from back home," he said. "Don' never sound right in English."

Mildred, forever clueless, accepted the explanation.

He then turned to Dad. "Yeah, I go," he said. "We worry about gettin' home later, when it comes. If it comes. Jus' like always, you find a way." Dad sat silently. He was touched by his cousin's pledge of faith, but he also felt its burden. It was clear the weight made him uneasy. He slowly shook his head. "Not like the ol' days, Leo," he said. "Now, the government's on us, tough as Joe Louis. I can' guarantee that . . ."

This time Uncle Leo shook his head. "Don' say that," he said, and leaned toward my father. He spoke in a loud whisper intended for Dad, but heard by all. "I been this land too long," he said, "and I don' believe much. But I believe you." He paused, staring at Dad. "Besides," he added, and he flashed a grin, "you a foreman. Big shot. You find a way."

Uncle Leo then sat back and reached into his jacket pocket to bring out a ragged wallet, which he opened and placed on the table. "Got maybe two hundred thirty bucks," he said. "That includes four fifties."

He pulled out four fifty-dollar bills and dealt one to each of us. "Take 'em," he said simply. Mildred and Stephanie pounced; their shares of the bounty quickly vanished. That left two. Mine just sat there. Dad had first to approve this large a transaction and, from the scowl on his face, it wouldn't pass.

"Leo!" Dad barked, "Wha' the hell . . ."

"Never mind, Manong," Uncle Leo said sharply. His tone surprised me. Before, he'd seemed so timid, so much like me whenever I had to face my father.

I realized something. Dad's ferocity was tied to his powerful and protective image. And Uncle Leo had a right to insist that Vince behave as he always did. Maybe Dad did, too. I filed that moment away, taking hope in the possibility that the meek weren't entirely powerless.

"Peanuts," Uncle Leo said. "Kept enough to cover room and board till we go. Like I said, I go with you."

He put his right index finger on the bill in front of Dad and pushed it toward him. "Take it, Manong," he said.

"No," Dad said. "I take you, not your money."

Uncle Leo smiled. "Tha's all I want," he said. He then pushed Dad's bill toward me—that made two! "For the boy."

Although unsure of the total, I knew the amount was huge. I fondly studied the stranger etched in green, whose acquaintance I soon hoped to make. It wasn't George Washington, who was worth twenty Hershey Bars. But I still needed Dad's okay before I could reach to gather in the loot. From him, no words—just a sigh and a roll of the eyes skyward—but it was enough. "Thanks Uncle Leo!" I said, as my right hand swept the table.

Uncle Leo suddenly turned toward Mildred and whispered something I couldn't hear, which she acknowledged with a nod.

"Buddy," she smiled, "your uncle Leo just reminded me that Stephie's got a recital about a mile from here, at her music teacher's, and wouldn't it be nice if you could go."

The thought appalled me—more time with Stephanie, her manicured mother, and her accordion music! I preferred the company of my father and uncle, even here in this nicotine haze. Yet, for the sake of propriety, I couldn't object. I just pretended not to hear, a veneer soon pierced by Dad's voice.

"Sure, he'll go," he said. "Why not?"

Traitor. But all wasn't lost. Uncle Leo had turned the tables on my father. Maybe I could, too, though not verbally, as Leo had done; that took an adult's confidence, something I lacked. Instead, I shot him a look: my best sad-face, deepened (I hoped) with shadows of betrayal.

I missed.

"I'll jus' pick 'im up later," Dad said. "I know the place."

The look having failed me, I rose, resigned to an afternoon of boring women and bad music. Stephanie and her mother were already near the door, while I still dawdled by the booth, hoping for a reprieve.

Dad grabbed my arm. "Sorry, Buddy," he said, "but it's been a long time for your uncle and me. We got things to catch up on, men only, and it jus' don' sound right in English."

"Ah, Dad," I said, trying hard not to whine. "I won't bother you, I promise. And besides, I don't understand Cebuano."

That little lie triggered in my father an odd smile. "Listen, Buddy," he said. "Maybe you don' understand. But you're my boy, and that means you listen real good and you're smart." He then pulled me close and whispered: "And what you maybe heard, you didn'—okay?"

Standing near the door were Mildred and Stephanie, subjects of a discussion in Cebuano that now had never happened. Dad laughed and pushed me in their direction.

Case closed. I paused before starting down the path to a dull and musically discordant afternoon, wondering how I could best feign interest. One solution, partial at best: I'd imitate my father, his demeanor, his arrogant gait, the latter complete with puffed-out chest and eyes focused straight ahead. I took one careful, choreographed step, then a second, but a third was halted by familiar voices and the sounds of laughter. I stopped.

Spoken Cebuano, its tones soft and melodious even from the tongues of men. I turned in time to see a stream of white smoke start to form a small cloud over their booth, a telltale sign marking the boundaries of a world I didn't want to leave.

Rico

When I was growing up in Seattle, Rico Divina was the baddest Filipino I ever knew, and I knew them all. Vietnam killed him. Not there, but it killed him nevertheless.

The last time I really saw him was August 1967, just before the start of my senior year in high school. I never thought those days would seem as distant and foreign as Burma, or Myanmar as some now call it, or even Vietnam. I was almost seventeen then, and Rico was a little more than a year older. We were both just starting to peer beyond the boundaries of the poor neighborhood that tied us down but also protected us and made us strong. It was home to Rico and me, and in my view, he ruled it.

Like many Filipinos, Rico was short and wiry, but he made up for it by being strong, fast, and clever—traits that earned respect even from the bloods, and they were always the hardest to impress.

White girls were a lot easier. He made them his specialty, particularly the long-legged blondes with ratted hair and heavy makeup. There were always a few at the weekly dances at the community center on Empire Way, hiding in the shadows of the dimly lit halls, their pale skin and high bouffants shining like beacons in the dark.

Rico would always show up at dances alone, resplendent in his tight black slacks, matching black jacket, and felt hat with a narrow—the bloods called it "stingy"—brim. He also wore pointed Italian boots and a pink shirt with a high collar pressed to a sharp, thin edge. All that was missing was the Cadillac, which he wanted but couldn't come close to affording. So he arrived by bus, riding it like the prince of public transportation. I knew he didn't have a car, but it made no difference to the girls he left with, even if they had to pay their own fare.

According to Rico he was bestowing a favor. They were in it for the danger, he explained.

Filipinos always hired black bands; they carried a horn section in addition to two guitarists and a drummer. The extra section shrank each musician's share of the profit. But no matter; this was black music, not white, and the horns made it raw and powerful, something white bands could never do.

Rico loved the horns and the sweating black angels who played them. They were his rhythm-and-blues heralds, and once they kicked in on a tune, he'd scan the room and choose his partner. He never said anything, just looked at his girl for the night and nodded in the general direction of the dance floor. Invariably she would follow, because she knew who Rico was and she understood the rules. Out on the floor she could move and match the rhythm, and maybe even do it really well, as some white girls who were trying to pass for something else were able to do. But it was Rico's show, and he was its dark star.

If the music was slow, he'd hold the girl tight and softly sing the lyrics of lost or impossible love. With the horns setting the mournful mood, he'd roll her rhythmically with his right thigh between her legs, using it like a rudder to guide her, inches off the floor, as he leaned back. I told him once that I could always tell his dance partners; they walked funny, like they'd spent the day on horseback.

Rico changed with the song. To an upbeat tempo he'd skate

halfway across the hall on one leg like James Brown, never a single pomaded hair ever out of place. He'd stop suddenly and do the splits, from which he'd just as suddenly rise to continue his journey to the other side. He defied gravity, just like James.

And just like James, his most obvious talents weren't suited for college. He had other skills, other potentials, but by the time public school was through ignoring him, I'm sure he wasn't sure what they were or even that they were.

Rico could dance and he could woo white girls. And there was one other thing: the boy could box. He was still an amateur, but the old guys like Tommy said he had "pro" written on the knuckles of both hands. Tommy, a part-time manager, also ran the Masonic Gym in downtown Seattle where Rico worked out. He'd once been a decent pro fighter, but, as Rico had put it to me, that must have been years ago, before electricity and pan-fried pork chops had turned his belly into mush. Fighting was something well-adjusted white folks didn't understand, but it was what the kids in my neighborhood did. Or even if they didn't, they thought about it all the time. I was more the thinking type, unlike Rico. As far back as I could remember, my mom had said: Think of your future, get an education, go to college. The future, from the day I began to read, was my own map. For Rico, Tommy was the first one to point him to a future, but the map, it turned out, was Tommy's.

The last time I saw Rico, he was honing his skills on a scared-looking Mexican kid in the small ring at the Masonic. I went down there that day because I'd heard a rumor that Rico had enlisted. He'd never said anything to me about it, and I wanted to find out.

I walked in at the split second Rico threw a perfectly timed right-hand counter at his opponent's head that, even with head-gear and fat sparring gloves, managed to knock the kid hard against the ropes. It was the kind of punch that loosens your eyeballs and rolls them back under your brain. It was even more devastating because Rico threw it just as the Mexican was leaning into his own jab, the effect being doubled because he came onto the punch.

Rico, the old-timers said, was a natural counterpuncher. It's a rare gift that the boxing gods give to a few which allows them to attack when they sense an opening created by an opponent's offensive move. Rico had again displayed his gift; the sound of the punch, his perfect form, the sharp backward snap of the Mexican's head followed by his body's collapse into the straining ring ropes, all testified to it. The blurred sequence of events, witnessed by myself and the small circle of Masonic regulars, drew our collective "ooh."

We all knew an assassin was at work and, like any good assassin, Rico knew his work wasn't done. Seeing the Mexican draped helplessly against the ropes with his hands down was too good an invitation. He almost skipped like a schoolgirl to close the distance between himself and his prey, and he held his right hand back a bit more than usual. He had enough torque in that right to launch his victim on a straight trajectory, like one of Henry Aaron's line drives, to some southern point where Spanish was spoken. I knew it, and evidently Tommy did, too. Quickly, and despite his girth, Tommy scrambled into the ring and slid like a fat snake in what he had to know was a vain attempt to beat Rico to his launching spot. "Stop!" he screamed from his prone position as the right-hand rocket took off.

"Goddammit!" Tommy muttered a second later, still on the canvas. The Mexican's torso sagged deep into the taut ropes that

strained and flung him face forward onto the canvas. The kid
was out even before he landed on his nose and lips, not his landing gear of choice, around which a pool of blood quickly started
to form. At the side of his face lay his mouthpiece, knocked
loose by the impact.

Tommy was livid. He just lay there for a second, stunned and
furious, looking at the prostrate body; his assistants, armed with
smelling salts and towels, were already entering the ring. The
old man rose, positioning himself close to Rico and in front of
him. "Get outta' here!" he screamed, flapping his stubby arms
for emphasis, slapping them repeatedly against his sides. With
each smack, his heavy tits shook more than a stripper's. I started
to giggle; he looked like he was trying to fly.

"You got it," Rico said calmly as he turned to go.

"And don't come back," Tommy added.

"Got that too," Rico said as he climbed between the ring ropes.
He paused, one leg in the ring, the other out, and turned toward
Tommy. "Too much garlic in that last batch of chops," Rico said
in the same flat tone. "Smell like a gypsy queen."

"You're outta' here!" Tommy screamed, stung by the truth.

Rico started to walk toward the dressing room. "Startin' to
look like one too, fatso," he said without looking back, but loud
enough to be heard.

It wasn't the first time Tommy had yelled at Rico for losing
control, for fighting instead of sparring. But I thought this really
might be it—not because Tommy wouldn't take him back, a fight
manager almost never turns away a potential moneymaker, and
Tommy loved my friend's talent more than he loved pork chops—
but because Rico himself had decided it was over. He wanted to
leave with a bang. That was his way.

I wondered what he'd have to say as I followed him back to

the dressing room. I opened the door slowly and saw him in the dim light, sitting on a stool, slumped in front of his locker. The cool of the room collided with the heat from his body, creating steam that covered him like morning fog. It was a little eerie. I stood by the door, waiting for him to turn and speak or do something to bring us back to more familiar terrain.

Finally, he looked over his shoulder and nodded at me. It wasn't much of a sign, but it was enough for the moment. "Goin' up in smoke, buddy," I said, trying to sound steady.

Rico paused and looked at himself. He chuckled. "Sure am," he said.

"What happened?"

"Fucker uppercut me," he said, "but Tommy didn't do shit. He knows the rules for sparring. Break clean. No cheap shots. Goddam Tommy. Can't count on him for nothin'." Rico pointed to a discolored spot on his neck. "That fucker nailed me," he said angrily. "He wanted to fight, so I fought. Nailed him back, too. Stapled his face to the floor."

I nodded. Rico laughed at the thought. The laugh almost put me at ease. I raised the question that had brought me to the gym in the first place. "I heard, man," I said quietly. "True story?"

There was no answer.

"Your mom called my mom and she don't want you to . . ."

Rico interrupted me, staring at the floor as he spoke. "Can't help it," he said. "Got nothin' goin' here."

It was the answer I didn't want to hear. I glanced around the room looking for someplace to sit. I felt heavy, like a bunch of men each the size of Buddha had jumped on my back and stayed there. I spotted a bench across the room and walked toward it.

"Damn," I said to myself as I sat down and buried my face in my hands. I'd known a lot of Filipinos from the neighborhood.

Most were drafted; some enlisted. Most went to Vietnam. Some returned; others didn't. I knew our time was coming. That's just the way it was, and I accepted it. We all did. In that sense, we were like our fathers and uncles who had fought in Europe or in the Pacific—and if they were lifers, in Korea, too. Like them, we asked no questions; couldn't even think of one to ask, much less expect an answer. For us, Vietnam had no moral ambiguities; the government called, and we went. Simple as that.

We vaguely hated communism, although we didn't know why. Fats Domino/the domino theory; knew one/heard about the other. Maybe related, but we weren't sure how. I didn't learn until much later that boys from poor neighborhoods like ours carried the flag into dangerous places for powerful, arrogant, and profoundly foolish old white men. But that was later. At sixteen I thought I'd go, too. I just wanted Rico to wait for us to do it together.

"Had to, Buddy," he said, using my nickname and interrupting my morose reverie. "Got no school. Got no job. Ain't colored, so I ain't got no black power let-your-hair-grow-out-don't-conk-it shit." I looked at him blankly. "What we got?" Rico asked angrily, referring to Filipinos in general and himself in particular. He got that way sometimes when he talked about his future, the one he was sure he didn't have. Rico stared at me straight and hard.

I scratched my head and scrambled; I wanted to throw a curve and back him off. "White girls," I finally said. " 'Specially blondes, tall long-legged ones."

Rico's laugh broke the momentum I'd thought was building to an uncomfortable point. "Yeah," he said, grinning. "Devil bitches, but I love 'em. Most bloods don't mess with 'em now, 'ceptin Sammy Davis." He smirked, then shrugged. "Leaves more for me," he said finally.

I felt confident enough to try to turn it serious again.

"Rico," I said quietly. "Don't go, at least not yet. There's ways.
. . you know, deferments. White guys do it all the time. Like
marriage . . ."

He shook his head no and looked at me like I'd lost it.

"Like college. . ." I said, trying again. I knew I was grasping,
and I knew he knew.

He rolled his eyes. "Yeah, like I'm a perfect candidate, a
goddam summa, whatever."

I was making no points and was getting a little desperate.
"Your mom," I blurted.

That hit home. He gave me no quick answer. "I love her," he
said finally. "But I'm eighteen, I'm signed, and I'm gone. The
Marines own my butt now, not Mama."

So it was over. I knew then he'd closed the matter before I'd
even had the chance to open it. I felt the Buddhas get heavier,
and I sagged just a bit more.

Rico sensed this and tried his best to cheer me up. He smiled.
"Hey, man, every Flip wants a gunfight," he said with bravado.
"You know, our heroic dick-expandin' tradition, more shit to impress the ladies with and tell our kids and grandkids." His effort
to cheer me didn't work. Undeterred, he tried another route. "I
thought about leavin' and what I'd leave you," he said solemnly
as he reached into his training bag. He found what he was looking for and handed it to me; it was a small black book. I looked
at the book and reached to take it.

"Man, what's this?"

Rico feigned surprise. "Yo' mama raise you in a cave or
somethin'? That book there's my address book—full of white
girls, 'specially blondes. Ain't gonna be needin' it where I'm
goin'. Gettin' me a new one anyway, full of Vietnamese writin'

and female Vietnamese names." He mimed a drum roll with his hands. "I'm changin' my taste," he said. "Expandin' my horizons to find new pussy, goin' like Columbus where no Flip's ever been . . ."

"Damn, man, all right, okay," I said sharply, interrupting him. Rico was starting to talk trash I didn't want to hear.

He seemed to notice, or at least that's what I thought. "I've had this book a long, long time," Rico then said, sounding dead serious. It was hard to tell with him, but going to war wasn't a trifling thing, so I gave him the benefit of the doubt. Wrong move. I was tricked like a trout rising to a fisherman's fly.

"I got it years ago," he went on, fixing me with a sharp look. My intense focus told him I was hooked; it was all he needed to know. He paused dramatically before reeling me in. "Before my first shorthair," he said in a near whisper. His deadpan continued. "What the shit," he said as he shrugged his shoulders. "A boy's gotta' dream."

I couldn't help smiling, despite my sudden irritation and sense of impending loss. Rico didn't miss a step.

"That book there," he said, and he repeated himself for emphasis, "that book there even got a name." It was too late. Like always, it was his dialogue, just like it was always his dance. I was his straight man and had to play along. I sighed. "What is it, man?" "Ho's I Know," he said, with a master's timing. Rico studied me, looking at my face for a sign of reaction. I didn't give him any. To my mind, this was too serious a moment.

"Oh," I said flatly. I held back and gathered my thoughts before speaking again. "So this is it?" I asked. I listened to myself uttering the words, creating the accusatory question. I'd miss him, which was all the more reason to keep the tone even. In our neighborhood, emotion was for sissies and not to be shown, even to friends. I thought I'd succeeded. I guess I hadn't.

"Hey," Rico said. "It ain't forever." His voice was softer. I looked at him closely and knew this time he wasn't setting me up.

"Man, come on by tonight," I said hopefully. "My folks, dinner . . . you know, a righteous goodbye."

"Can't."

For Rico, "can't" never meant "maybe." I pressed him, though, because I figured I had nothing to lose. I unloaded both barrels, or tried to.

"The folks, man," I started, "they . . . ."

"Can't," he said again, with a firmness that ended any further appeal to my parents' affection. He looked at me and didn't speak until he was convinced I got the message. "Look," he said finally. "Got some time before I report and I'm gettin' outta' town, maybe to Frisco. Ain't never been there and I'd kinda' like to go, you know, like Cookie tried to."

Cookie was our friend, a young black kid we'd grown up with. All he talked about, once he figured out his dick wasn't just for pissing, was getting laid. He didn't care whether the girls were black, white, yellow, whatever—a fact attested to by his multicolored progeny and their angry grandparents who universally threatened to harm him. All he cared about was a girl's attitude, which he hoped was enthusiastic, and finding more eligibles and more places to hide.

Cookie knew Seattle was too small; he kept bumping into relatives of his lovers who wanted to kill him. The last, the brother of a Chinese girl, shot at him but missed. His frustrated assailant shouted at the fleeing Cookie that sooner or later he'd turn him into a barbecue slab and hang him from a hook. The image of his glazed flank hanging in the front window of a Chinatown restaurant frightened Cookie, and he decided it was time to go. He had to figure out where, and thought he'd discovered Heaven when he read about San Francisco and its sexual revolution.

When I last saw him he was growing his hair out, and I listened while he recited a litany of black-power phrases. He explained he was going to San Francisco to poke a commune full of white middle-class hippie girls who, by doing his black butt, would think they were promoting social justice. He'd figured it out. But just as he was about to leave, his draft notice came. Cookie died in Vietnam and never made it to Freakin' Frisco.

Rico didn't want to make the same mistake; I knew he had a good reason to leave, so I backed off and let the matter drop. He must have known I'd surrendered, and that giving up wasn't easy.

"Look," he said kindly, "it's hard, 'specially 'cause you and me are like this." He clenched his fist to illustrate. "You know, tight like brothers."

I looked at him and nodded agreement, feeling too sad to reply. "Guess this is it," I said, as I extended my hand. "Better get goin'."

He took my hand, pulled me toward him, and hugged me awkwardly. "Look," he said as he released me a moment later. "You're smart and you're goin' to Catholic school . . . college prep and takin' trig, Buddy. Me, I took shop, and it's the shop guys that's goin'. If the shit's still on in a year from now, get your butt in college. At least you can cut a deal, and if you go you'll be an officer with a safe job and a desk. Don't do like I'm about to do and go put yourself in a box."

He was silent for a minute, maybe more, but I knew it would end. I waited. He stared at the floor and breathed heavily. When he broke the silence, the tone of his voice was like a sudden hard jab, and so was his choice of words.

"Damn," he muttered without looking up. "Damn," he said again, louder this time, looking at me. "We're like brothers, you know, but we're different. 'Cause I'm the one that's gotta go."He paused again before speaking. "Buddy, you got hope. You got hope without ever havin' to leave town."

I was stunned and even unnerved. I wasn't sure if the anger in his voice was aimed at me or his situation. "Rico," I said, without really knowing what to say next. "I . . ."

"Better leave, man," he said, cutting me off. "We're cool, but I need to be alone. Gotta sort it out."

I just stared at him, blanked out by this new face on my old friend. I froze and stayed seated because I couldn't accept what I was hearing.

He returned my stare. "Man, you understand English?"

I did, and this time his tone—curt, cold, full of menace—made me rise and begin to take the first steps of my backward shuffle toward the door. I knew that tone well. I'd heard it directed at scores of childhood enemies, but I'd never thought I'd be the target.

He was no longer looking at me, but as I retreated I never took my eyes off him. To this day I'm not sure if it was for fear of what he might do, or for love of a friend I might never see again. I backed through the doorway, and as I did so, Rico became a picture in a frame, a sepia photo, an image in a seam of memory. Through the dim light, I saw him motionless, leaning forward, head bowed, this man with the moves. A seam of memory. Without a word to anyone, I walked out of the gym.

The Second Room

In 1967 I joined the Jun Fan Gung Fu Institute in Seattle, more commonly known as the Bruce Lee school, and stayed for thirteen years. By then Bruce had left for Hollywood. But the school he'd founded stayed open, put in the care of Taky Kimura, his good friend and former student. Taky carried out his mentor's wishes, like the decision not to advertise. Bruce was about fighting, not the size of yellow-page ads. Although the school was open to the public, it wasn't advertised. Students learned of it by word of mouth. Nothing commercial, just the way Bruce wanted.

Consistent with that theme, the instructors weren't paid. Almost three decades later it's still the same. Neither Taky, nor his assistant, Roy Hollingsworth, nor anyone else who taught there has ever made a dime. It was payment enough to be part of a legend.

And the style they taught—Jeet Kune Do—wasn't pretty or mysterious, just simple and effective. Unlike most Chinese martial arts with their twirling, leaping choreographed forms, we kept our balance and stayed on the ground. We never sought our higher selves; Zen was never spoken.

Back then the school, because it was open, was always exciting and sometimes dangerous. A thirty-buck fee covered rent and equipment but didn't include background checks or psychiatric exams for the cross section of Seattle who showed up to train. The month before I joined, two senior students had been expelled for fighting each other. Their dispute, starting in class, was settled outside. One of them, a black belt *judoka*, later turned to amateur boxing. Within six months, he was the heavyweight runner-up in the Seattle Golden Gloves. His opponent became a cop who later found Jesus in the joint after he'd killed his wife, my grade-school classmate. He was released, I heard, and killed again, Jesus's presence notwithstanding.

The expulsions governed our conduct. Because we wanted to stay, we stopped just short of full-blown fights. But everything else was okay, which made the atmosphere electric—almost, but not quite, out of control. In that sense, the school resembled the African plain, its hierarchy denoting predators and prey. Rookies were prey—numerous, nervous, defenseless—expected to take lumps from senior students who stalked us and threw punches we couldn't parry, kicks we couldn't block. We were their training dummies for action on the street, but better, because we could react and show pain. Still, no one complained, not even the most abused rookie. Pain, we figured, was a small price to pay just to be there.

Although I stayed at the school for thirteen years, learning from Taky and others who taught me, and from those whom I later taught, the key block of time for me was those first few months. Taky was mostly absent. His world had been shaken by the back-to-back deaths of two older brothers. That meant the burden of the family-owned grocery, the First Hill IGA, fell solely on him.

In this formative period, Roy was my teacher and model, my *sifu*. I first saw him at the IGA on the day I went to introduce myself to Taky. As I searched the store, I passed Roy, who was wearing the mark of his trade, a butcher's blood- stained smock.

He was standing in an aisle, deep in conversation. Although I didn't know who he was, I noticed him because, when he spoke, his body moved to merge words with motion; his gestures brought attention to a pair of long arms and the reach of his thick, calloused hands.

Roy taught me the basics: the salutations that begin and end each class, stance and balance, kicks and punches. What amazes me still is how simple and practical it all was. Like the stance: no contortions and exotic poses, no rigid stances or imitations of legendary animals. Just hands up, with the right hand and leg forward, the latter covering the groin, body weight balanced. Simple.

"Like a boxer fighting southpaw?" I asked.

"Precisely."

Roy should know. He'd fought as an amateur in England, and later as a pro in Chicago; he carried the marks of his old trade, especially above his eyes and on the flat bridge of his nose. Although years from the ring, he still had a fighter's instincts and skills. In addition, he'd chalked up stints as a teenage British paratrooper fighting Malayan Communists, and later as a professional soccer player. Roy didn't need Bruce Lee to be deadly. But Lee's talent was such that he converted all, even the dangerous ones. Until he met Bruce, Roy had dismissed martial arts as harmless. "Useless," he declared. "Can't slip a jab or block a hook, at least not mine. Ah, but that Bruce . . ."

Then there were the kicks—nothing above the belt, movie fights notwithstanding. Kneecaps and shins were favored. Easy to reach, easy to hurt. Damn, I thought, why hadn't I thought of that? Finally, the punches. Short and quick—exploding in a crossing and recrossing motion through an imaginary lengthwise line splitting the body in half.

"Think in flurries, not a single big punch," he advised. "And when you throw, move into the man quick and hard. Beat him to that center line, take away his room to punch. That way he has to go around you. It's called 'closing the gap.' If you do that, you'll whip him every time."

At least, that's what he said. Closing the gap with a straight punch was our basic style, one learned by every rookie during the first few weeks. You moved onto the man and kept moving until you dropped him. Simple and effective. But in watching Roy spar, I noticed that he didn't always follow his own advice. To our orthodox straight punch arsenal, he added boxing staples—hooks, jabs, uppercuts, crosses—all to deadly effect. After one such show, I asked him why he mixed boxing moves with the straight punch.

Roy smiled and shrugged. " 'Cause they work," he said simply. "That's one thing about Lee. He knows everyone's different, everyone's got a different strength. You figure it out and build your style around it. You learn the basics here, but everything else you pick up on your own. Just keep what works for you, not for me or Taky, but for you. For me, boxing still works, like second nature. But for you, who knows? As you get on, you'll learn moves, techniques. But you gotta always ask: Does it work?"

It was a hell of a question, an antidote to orthodoxy or smugness. Although Bruce Lee's physical skills dazzled the public, his skepticism moved me more. In surveying the ritualized attacks of the traditional Chinese fighting arts, he saw weaknesses—artificial moves that didn't work, not on the street. His critique led him to rebel not just against those arts, but against the sterile weight of Chinese opinion and tradition that sustained them. His answer stressed simpler moves, functional in a crisis, aimed at addressing one question: Does it work?

I've carried that hard question with me ever since. I applied it first to martial arts—training sessions, boxing rings, and street fights (short punches, uppercuts, and hooks work)—and eventually beyond to religion, marriages, and careers. Asking the question can be lonely. There are few models. In asking it, history matters less (so-and-so did it, and you can, too) than personal experience and a short supply of wisdom. But each choice I've made has always followed that question, that troubling inquiry first raised almost thirty years ago.

I couldn't get enough. At home, I'd train with friends, family, alone; it didn't matter. I'd spend hours before a mirror checking for precision, position, and speed, trying to beat my image to the punch. Learning to fight became an obsession, another way to gain respect.

My neighborhood, the Central District, was mostly black but was dotted throughout with pockets of Filipinos. In one of those pockets, my family and I lived. The sixties hit the neighborhood hard; people started to draw lines and call each other down, just on race. Mostly the conflict was black and white, but where did that leave me? For a while I put it aside, confident in knowing that, at least on my street, I had respect. That's what mattered. In my world, you could never have too much. Respect—the most precious currency of the poor and colored. It couldn't pay the note, but it might buy a walk past older men who'd check you out. They'd nod. "You bad," the nod said. Relieved, you'd nod back. Some got respect by fighting; others got it through sports. I'd chosen the latter route, spending summer hours at the outdoor hoops of Madrona playfield, where every evening the best players in the city gathered. Most were older—college players, legends, could've beens—and all were black, except me. In this world, respect could only be found in the lane, faking left and driving right, or reversing it the next time around. I'd ignore the outside jumper—a safe and sissy suburb move—and take it hard to the hole, defying big sullen brothers who enjoyed swatting trespassers back to their moms. If I survived, and sometimes I didn't, it was defense chest to chest and grabbing boards in traffic. From the fellas at Madrona I earned respect. But the playground was just a small part of the Central Area, not to mention the city and the world beyond. As Seattle grew more tense, I wondered: Off my street, among those who didn't know me, would my record at Madrona matter?

Probably not. I figured then I'd better learn to fight. But from whom? My father, Vince, was a possibility, but we were too different. He was a tough man and, unlike me, quick tempered, made that way by twenty-five years of migrant work. Although Dad had left the fields, the anger remained and drove his skill. As a kid, I came to hate walking anywhere with him. Hard looks or insults, real or imagined, could set him off. Dad could've taught me, but how do you teach anger? I never asked him.

So I tried a succession of different martial arts schools, the last being one that taught a traditional Chinese style. Somewhere in the middle of futility—between the first mechanical punch thrown from a squat and rigid deep-horse stance, plus thousands more—I realized this was useless, a point underscored by Sal, a neighborhood acquaintance.

He mocked my style with words, and worse—with quick jabs and hooks I couldn't defend. My moves were wooden, hands too low, too slow. I'd paid forty bucks a month and couldn't stop a jab, not even when he told me it was coming. That day I blocked more than one with my face and forehead. Sal took pity.

"Remember Kato?" he asked.

I nodded. "Yeah," I said sullenly. Of course. Who could forget?

By then Bruce Lee was on his way to becoming the baddest man on film. Ever. He started out as Kato, the only reason to watch *The Green Hornet* on the tube. As Kato, Bruce didn't move so much as he exploded on opponents. Sure, the fights were staged, but no one could fake Lee's balance and swift, balletic fluidity—better, I thought, than Ali's best—or the speed of his kicks and punches, either hand. All of that was real enough. He was already a legend. Much like Michael Jordan to another generation, the laws of nature that restrict and limit didn't apply, at least not to him. He was one bad dude.

"You're no Kato," he laughed.

What could I say? I quit the school and saved my money, swearing to spend it on something better.

It almost never came. Finding the Bruce Lee school was a fluke that turned on a tip from Rick, a high-school buddy who worked nearby, a part-time checker at the First Hill IGA. One afternoon, Rick mentioned in passing that his boss, Taky Kimura, was Bruce Lee's friend and student, and that Taky ran the school Bruce had founded. I begged him to set me up. He shrugged. No sweat. Simple as that.

Over time, I came to know other students, to gauge their skills and temperaments. Some were sane, decent folks. Some were not. And of the last, the most dangerous were those with skill. They were older, bigger, stronger—a bad combination if you were new. Typically we'd work in pairs, with rookies matched against senior students. For many of the latter, a training session was a green light for bullying, and the most vicious aggressor was a stocky, powerful man we rookies nicknamed "Killer." If we beginners were victims, he was our main tormentor, needlessly punishing his unskilled partners, leaving welts on sternums, stomachs, and foreheads. Killer worked construction, and he often wore his work boots to class, not tennis shoes, knowing full well that his choice of footwear made blocking his potent kicks more painful.

Supervising our slaughter was Roy. He'd move from pair to pair, making suggestions, inspecting technique. His mere presence protected us, slowed aggressors down. "Easy now," he'd say, a phrase that brought respite until he moved on.   But even then, a predator would sometimes go too far—maybe a rookie's head snapped back too hard, or his body doubled over. If Roy noticed, he'd intervene, talk to the suspect, tell him to cool it. "Come on," he'd scold. "It's too easy. You don't need to do that."

Sometimes, however, talking didn't work; the bully would remain unrepentant. We prayed for such defiance, barrels of it, because Roy would then offer to spar with him, an invitation designed to induce repentance. It gave us hope and underscored another lesson from the African plain: badness is relative. And Roy was the baddest of all. But unlike Killer and our other tormentors who beat beginners for sport, Roy never did. He didn't have to. Unlike our predators, he'd long since faced the pain and fear of the prize ring to become a man with nothing to prove.

At 185 pounds, Roy had a heavyweight's power and a smaller man's speed. That meant he could plow right through a foe, or, if he chose, could stay outside and pick his shots. Either worked; often, he'd do both. At the start, he might probe, play, and even drop his hands while slipping single punches or straight punch flurries. In this phase, he'd just defend with old boxing tricks— rolling with punches, tucking his cheek against his shoulder— all designed to show he couldn't be touched, must less hurt. It was a devastating display. Then, tired of the game, he'd launch his offensive—boxing jabs and crosses, straight punches, grabs and traps, a whole volley of techniques—with such precision, power, and malice that his foe, our tormentor, was suddenly befuddled, weak, and vulnerable, just like us.

If Roy was really irritated, he'd add short, punishing hooks, hard to defend against. These he threw with an open hand—so as not to kill, just plant a lesson—with brain-jarring slaps upside the head. First the right—bip—then the left—bop. Then maybe again—bip-bop—for good measure. After that, Roy wouldn't say much, didn't have to. Lesson learned. We were safe until the next class.

Although Roy was our protector, there were some tasks he couldn't do. The achievement of skill is, at its core, an individual prize. Unlike Roy, I was just starting out, unsure of myself and a bit apprehensive. And fueling my doubt was a second room in the school, adjoining the main one, where pairs of students, senior matched against rookie, entered to spar—hard. I'd never been through its doors, but I'd heard a lot.

"In there," one student said, "almost anything goes. Long as it works." He said they fought on a board about the size of a door, a primitive venue that forced flurries of quick, direct, explosive techniques. The action would stop only when a fighter was forced off the board. Roy and the other instructors rarely interrupted these matches, figuring I guess that a healthy dose of violence and fear was essential to progress, especially for rookies. From the main room, we could hear thuds and slaps, curses and screams. The noises made me nervous.

During a Friday session, a fellow who'd started a few weeks ahead of me had been taken to the room. He emerged bruised and shaken. "Rough," was all he said.

I knew I was next, probably on Monday when class reconvened. That left the weekend, too much time to nurse my growing fears and to doubt, for the first time, my nerve and dedication. Over the two-day break, my mind raced from scene ("You fought well," said one voice) to scene ("He's unconscious!" said another). I wondered how others had faced it, had focused the mind and summoned the anger. In seeking an answer, I quickly skipped over Roy. He wasn't a model. He'd fought too long, both inside the ring and out, and had come to know violence well. It didn't scare him.

I wondered if it had ever scared Taky. Because of the sudden deaths of his brothers, I'd seldom seen him and couldn't say I knew him well. I had only an impression, now months old, based on the meeting arranged by my friend, Rick. I thought back to that day.

One morning Rick had said okay, that after class Taky would meet me at the First Hill IGA, only three blocks from my high school. I'd passed the grocery store many times but had never paid it much attention. It was a small box-shaped building buried in a valley of tall, aging brownstones and new high-rises. In this neighborhood, abutting a bustling downtown, the IGA was easy to miss.

At the final bell, I raced out the door and down the street, stopping in the IGA parking lot to catch my breath and gain a semblance of composure. The semblance wasn't much, but having come this far, I decided to go on through the automatic door. I wondered how to introduce myself. What could I say to someone touched by legend?

Once in, I still wasn't sure. I stalled, strolling slowly through the store, practicing phrases inside my head. Near the meat section I had my first look at Roy. He was talking to another employee. As he spoke, his huge right index finger jabbed the air for emphasis.

I passed Roy and walked clear to the front. I felt as ready as I'd ever be and asked the clerk for Taky Kimura. She pointed toward the produce aisle, where a Japanese man was inspecting a table full of apples, oblivious to all but the apples themselves. He stood medium height and was stocky (the perfect build for a *judoka*, which I later discovered he once was), in his mid-thirties, maybe older, hard to tell.

My apprehensions were unfounded. Taky saw to that. After my first few mumbled words and his offer of an apple (quickly accepted), I felt at ease. A man lacking pretension, he answered all my questions. I was stunned a bit by the contrast of Taky's humility with Bruce's image of explosive arrogance. It seemed an odd match. But yes, he was Bruce's student. And yes, he ran a small Chinatown club across the street from the Four Seas, a restaurant I knew well. We covered topics (like school) beyond the martial arts. His interest, I felt, was genuine. He liked young people and seemed to like me. I was so comfortable I almost forgot the purpose of my visit. But when it came time to choose and align the right words, I balked. He acted as if he didn't notice that my face was starting to flush. "We'll meet tonight," he said. "If you're interested, come down to the school about seven." And so I did, many times over. Now, months later, I found myself balking again. I thought about Taky. His kindness had touched me. Such a trait, I assumed, sprang from loving parents and protective older brothers who formed a precious core around him that violence rarely touched. Yet this gentle,

considerate man was the head of a tough, rowdy school. He had
Bruce's respect, and Roy's too. Somewhere along the way, he
must have had to face a challenge similar to mine, and maybe
he'd had to beat down his fears, just like I was trying to do. Taky
had survived. Maybe I could, too.

My premonition proved true. Monday marked the start of my
fifth month of training. The session started innocently—exer-
cises, then technique drills. During the break, Roy motioned for
me. "You'll be working here tonight," he said, pointing to the
doorway to the second room. "I'll get you a partner."

Silently I entered the room for the first time. It was a bare,
narrow place, poorly lit by a single weak bulb that dangled from
a cord on the ceiling. My eyes adjusted to make out the form of
a door-sized board in the middle of the cement floor. Deep in my
belly, I could feel a knot form. I studied this tiny arena, ponder-
ing what techniques its dimensions might allow. Not many, I
concluded—just straight blasts, and hope like hell I'd give better than I'd take. A figure suddenly appeared in the doorway.
Even without good light, I knew who it was. Just his build alone—
starting with his thick, muscular neck—gave him away. It was
Killer. I hoped it was a mistake, that others would appear and
Killer would be paired with one of them. No one else showed.
Hope disappeared when he took his position on the board and
motioned for me to do the same. The knot tightened. Killer was
mine for the night.

For a solid hour he pounded me. I'd throw and occasionally
land, which surprised me but only angered him further, prompt-
ing quicker and harder hand and foot barrages, driving me backward off the board, again and again. Still, I'd return, resume my

position, and begin once more. Then I decided to try something new.

Till then, my attack had been orthodox. I had moved right down the middle, technically perfect, but foolish against Killer, whose build and disposition controlled this area via his straight punch flurries, quicker and more powerful than mine. This time, however, as Killer started his rush, I stepped back and faded slightly to the right. I just managed to avoid his oncoming left, over which I threw a right hook, tight and fast like the bombs Roy threw. Bip. It landed hard upside Killer's head, surprising him. Surprising me, too, as I forgot to bop with the left. Killer, like any good fighter, pounced on this lapse to renew his bruising attack and drive me once more off the board.

Bent over, hands resting on knees, I stalled for time. The pain in my arms and chest throbbed in new spots to which I wasn't anxious to add. I glanced up and saw Killer pacing the board, slowly, steadily, hands on his hips, eager to beat me again. Strategies raced through my mind—straight punch? (he was too strong); another hook? (it worked, but he'd just seen it); take a dive?   Killer was pacing faster now. I sighed. I was still undecided, but I joined him on the board, ready for the worst.

"That's it," said a loud voice, ending my torment. Roy was standing in the dim light by the doorway. As I passed him on the way to the main room, he pulled me aside. "You're coming along," he said.

"Thanks, *sifu*," I replied.

"Nice hook," he said with a smile. "Keep it. It works for you. But you gotta follow up." He paused. "Not too rough, was it?"

I could feel the bruises on my arms and upper torso. My belly was tender; my thighs had taken so many kicks I could barely walk. "Nah," I lied.

"That's a good boy," he said.

I went to a corner of the room for the salutation marking the end of class. As we lined up, I looked around and studied the faces of those newer than I. I smiled. Food for their predators— a state as natural as life on the African plain, or the second room in the Bruce Lee school.

His brothers' deaths took a toll on Taky. Even as he mourned, the store stayed open, demanding more attention than anyone could imagine or pay. Something had to give; he eventually closed the Chinatown school, temporarily. When Taky and Roy reopened the school, it was in a different locale— the spacious basement of the First Hill IGA—and had a different approach. It was not a school open to the public. A few old students were invited back, including myself. Killer and the other lesser predators and lunatics were gone; there was no second room.

In this new, less hostile environment, we stressed techniques and conditioning and downplayed competition. We worked well together. Although some got hurt, the injury was always accidental, not the product of malice.

But even peace has its price. I began to miss the old days, the tension, the sense of challenge, even the fear. I started to prowl martial arts classes and boxing gyms looking for spars, eventually settling on the latter. I respected boxing's functional nature, an art less concerned with style than result, i.e., landing a punch that hurts the other guy.

In one bout, I fought a tall, rangy Navajo named Clyde. He was vicious and powerful, a raw talent who later turned pro. I'd seen him slaughter three other boxers; he'd played with them, hitting them just hard enough to keep them standing. When we hooked up, we were just supposed to spar lightly and focus on technique, nothing too heavy. That changed moments into the match as I slipped his hard, straight right designed to slam my forehead into my brain.

The spar was off; the fight was on. I got under him and smothered his power. I counterpunched and held, bobbed and weaved, hit him wherever, whenever I could. Legal and illegal tactics blurred; Clyde was too dangerous. I did whatever worked.

In the second round, frustrated by my lack of sportsmanship and his lack of success, Clyde made a stupid move. He lunged at me and missed, tangling his long arms in the ropes. Before the coach could intervene, I rushed over and hooked him hard on the back of his unprotected head. It was a good punch; my wrist and hand tingled from the impact.

Near the end of the bout, I'd managed another illegal but effective move. Trapping both of Clyde's hands with my left arm, I pinned them tight against my body. I was hooking him with my free right as the bell rang.

I smiled as I left the ring. I'd fought well and had parried or slipped most of his shots while landing almost all of mine. It was a great ratio, one I figured any fighter would've loved—even Killer or Roy.

August 1968

On the shaded bank I sat and stared at the narrow lagoon, its waters dark, deep, perpetually still, even when the winds came to stir the willows that covered its shores. Somewhere beyond, though not too far, were skylines and neighborhoods, cries of fear and anger. To this I'd return, but later. For now, it was just me and my special place. Secluded and safe, it served as shelter in Seattle, which, in the summer of '68, was a city seeking shelter from itself.

I knew the spot well, having discovered it eight years earlier at the end of a bike ride thirty minutes from my Central District home. At age ten, I had only a fishing pole and a cap full of hope. That afternoon I'd caught a small bass, staying long enough to watch shadows from the shore stretch across the water to end another summer day.

Over the years, I'd return, often with friends but sometimes alone, often to fish but sometimes, as now, just to watch. And to wonder at the constancy of its rhythm, especially now, in a city caught up in an age full of change.

Change. To Seattle it came in 1968, charging hard like a downhill train at this settled, complacent town. I saw it in my neighborhood, a quiet mix of blacks and Filipinos, among people I'd known for a lifetime. Their anger, black anger, the fuel that drove the revolution—and the response: white fear riding three cops to a car. But what about us, neither black nor white, who lived on the same block and shared the poverty? Did the revolution spare observers?

I had no answer as I moved toward the water's edge, my gloom broken by a sudden flash of green followed by a loud splash. Distracted, I smiled, watching the ripples reach the shore—a bass was chasing its elusive meal. This meant late afternoon, when waters were cooled by a jagged blanket of shade reaching from the far bank to where I stood. There was a second splash, then another. Soon the surface would roil with hungry predators and frightened, evasive prey. I glanced at my watch—five-thirty. Aaron, one of my best childhood friends, had called to say he wanted to talk. Important, he said. He'd be here in thirty minutes, time enough to sit, relax, and enjoy the unchanging late-day rhythm of this special place. The lagoon quickly filled with ripples and leaps tied by memories to my heart, making it race, and, in my thoughts, Aaron and I were kids again fishing the waters.

The surface, once so frenzied, turned suddenly still. Then suddenly more leaps, powerful upward thrusts, at each apex a midair pirouette that mocked gravity. The performers were two of the biggest bass I'd ever seen: tail-walkin' pole-breakin' trophies. Aaron and I hurriedly cast our lines to the centers of the splashes. A second later we pulled them in, laughing as older fishermen glared in envy. One of these, an old black man in faded blue coveralls, walked over to us. "Nice fish," he smiled. "Wha's you boys' secret?"

Aaron grinned at him. "Ain' no secret, mister. Me and my partner," he said, pointing at me, "we jus' havin' fun."

As he spoke, the sky began to darken, not from the sudden movement of clouds but from a sharp, gathering haze. I scanned the horizon. To the east, where our homes were, a thin line of black smoke rose lazily skyward. Alarmed, I tried to get my friend's attention, but by then he was in full debate on fishing minutiae: live bait or artificial lures, bass or trout. I tried subtlety, not wanting to be rude—head nods and hand signs, all useless.

"Worms and stink bait, boy," the old man said. "Works for me—been workin', too, near fifty years—and that's all that counts." He spoke solemnly, using age and a full, resonant Negro baritone to intimidate a twelve year old and win the point.

Aaron, who loved the skill of lures, didn't even flinch. "Mister, maybe for you," he said nonchalantly, "and don' mean no disrespect." He then pointed to his prized fish and set one more hook. "That fish there," he said evenly. "Caught it with a lure, and ain' no one can say it don' work."

That's the way he was. His carefree ways covered a mind that was always on. The old man didn't have a chance.

"Aaron," I said loudly. No reply. He was expanding the discussion, moving on to the merits of his favorite lures.

"Now, flatfish . . ."

He never finished the sentence. This time I yanked on his wrist so hard his head bobbed, and I added for good measure a scream that stopped hearts.

"Aaron!"

"Damn, Buddy," said a familiar voice. "Keep it down, man. Folks'll get the wrong idea, you screamin' my name. Damn. We close'n all, but I ain' yo' bitch."

I didn't even look, didn't have to. Aaron had been gone a year, courtesy of a scholarship for poor but promising colored folk. Same old Aaron, speaking the rude, loud patter of the street. Time in college, even a fancy one, hadn't refined him. I was glad.

Bloods spoke that way; Filipinos, too. That's how we grew up. But now we were young men, old enough to interest local draft boards. And although we had both become bilingual—over the years we'd learned how to speak to whites—when we got back home and together, we fell into our language of choice.

His serve, my volley. I smiled and fired back.

"Shoulda tol' me, brotha' man," I said slowly, "fo' you gave it up."

We shook hands. "Same old Buddy," he laughed. "Always tryin'."

"Uh huh," I nodded. "You was good, too. Girlfriend know about this? Better tell her, man . . ."

Dangerous words, used only against enemies—or friends, very good friends. Heads got busted for less. Still, I savored the score—bull's eye. He cringed, a sure sign to press on. "Take it there ain' no barbers back East. Say you get loaded, man, drop a roach on your head, a lit one, bury it in that nappy shit." I paused. "You my friend 'n all," I sighed, "but damn, man, you' a fire hazard."

First his manhood, then his hair. Music was next. "Whatcha think, man," I began solemnly. "I'ma put you on the spot: Beach Boys or Beatles? You gots an opinion. I know it. Surveyed the brothers on the corner, and they say the Boys, 'cause they American." Another pause. "Who say white folk can' jam?"

He'd have to come back and break my roll. "Buddy," Aaron finally said, interrupting me. He sounded meek, and with good reason. He was holding bottom ground, in this case somewhere near the mouth of a sewer with more shit on the way. "Same ol' no-fishin' Buddy," he went on with more confidence. "Turn around, boom, you out!"

Weak. Hangin' with rich, polite white kids had got him out of practice. So I let him slide. Besides, what could I say? It was true, all true, and had always been a source of mild childhood ridicule (mostly from him). Still, I was glad to see Aaron. We'd been friends since grade school, a bond cemented by time spent fishing these waters. Every summer, we'd walk or ride the three miles to fish our spot, sometimes five days straight. It would've stayed that way if I'd had a say. I didn't. When his folks divorced, Aaron and his mom moved across town, disrupting prematurely a lovely summer schedule I had never wanted to end.

Eventually, and like any boy reaching puberty, I found other interests. This left less time to fish, more time to navigate an awkward adolescence—complete with voice change, body hair, and overnight height that stole coordination. I liked my old self better but knew it was gone, sloughed off and sun dried like old snake skin. I figured I was stuck for the duration, however long that was (until sixteen, it turned out), and decided then to endure as best I could. Tomorrow would bring answers. But when it didn't, as was often the case, I'd go to the lagoon, sit on its bank, and fish waters that never changed.

Sometimes Aaron would come with me, catching the bus across town. On those rare days, we'd renew our friendship. Fishing this lagoon was the ritual that kept our bond current. We'd spend hours just catching up, then push ahead to bold points too distant from who we were. Under the willows, protected by shade, we traded secrets and dreams, often staying after dark. On these occasions, he'd dig in his pocket and flip me a dime. "Better call," he'd say. "We ain' done yet. Yo' mama get mad, tell her you were wit' me. We in this together."

The passing of summers also made it clear that, for a while, puberty had been kinder to him than to me. Only one year separated us, but during that span, it might as well have been ten.

He was quickly becoming a man of the world, or at least of a place grander than mine.

"Hey, blood," Aaron said on one occasion. "Got me some stank."

Stank? I didn't know the word, didn't know what he meant. Still, I felt pressure to keep up, to reply and seem wiser than I was. "Stank," I mumbled. "Yeah, stank."

"Fine bitch, too," he said. "Right there in her mama's house. She's older, three years or so. Ain' nothin' better'n older woman. Mama's fine, too. Gonna check her out next." He paused, smiling. "Hey, Buddy, ever get an older woman?"

His question presupposed prior experience, nonexistent at fourteen. I was caught in the grip of manchild stagnation, all pustules and the first sparse strands of facial hair. I went to Catholic school. Hey, I wanted to say. We don't do stank. An older woman? Any woman? I was lucky my mom still claimed me. My face flushed as his inquiry dangled, unanswered. I just stared at the water.

Fortunately, the lagoon granted a reprieve that lasted the rest of the day. "Damn!" he shouted, as a hungry bass rose to take his plug. After five minutes' combat against spirited leaps and dives, Aaron landed his fish, and, by day's end, three others.

I was less succesful, which was usually the case, but didn't care. Unlike Aaron, who skillfully deceived fish, I preferred a less taxing approach: worms, or marshmallows and eggs. That way I could bait a hook, drop it in the water, and forget about it until the bobber dipped or the pole twitched. While waiting on the bank, my attention would drift toward conversations, laughter, daydreams; an inevitable nap also filled each afternoon. "Man," Aaron had once scolded, waking me. "You here to catch fish?"

"Nah."

For me, being at the lagoon was reward enough; catching fish was incidental. Aaron was right. When I fished, I napped, and I saw nothing wrong with pairing the two.

"Hey, man," Aaron said, interrupting my stream of memories. Emboldened by my silence, he was again on the move. "I remember . . ." But not too far before I cut him off at the knees. "Needs my sleep, blood," I said. "It enhances my beauty, which, when I gets enough, I will donate to yo' needy ass." Another score. Didn't even have to look. Faking a yawn, I rolled over on my side. It was too easy. Aaron had been away too long, but he'd keep trying, and I'd keep shutting him down. It was time to change.

" 'Sides, man," I said, breaking the cycle, "wha's so important you gotta wake me in the first place?"

The shift surprised him. "Nothin'," he said.

"Then, sucka', what we doin' here?" I stared at him and spoke with a tone that said more abuse was on its way. "Man, I coulda been wit' yo'. . ."

"All right," he said evenly.

". . . girlfriend."

Aaron sighed. "God's truth, man. No more bullshit," he said. I smiled and nodded.

"Two nights ago I was hangin' wit' some brothers from the old neighborhood. You know, Marcus 'n them. Not doin' nothin', just hangin' down on Cherry near the school. It was hot, hot as the devil, but we was cool, just sippin' wine, mindin' our own business. When all of a sudden—boom—cops was goin' crazy. So many pigs, man, I ain' never seen. Flyin' by, I mean flyin' by. So me and my partners, we go check it out."

I knew the scene. Night before last, violence had erupted along 23rd Avenue, the heart of the Central District. From my house, about two miles away, I heard the sirens, saw the smoke. "Uh huh," I nodded. "Heard talk, blood. So I stayed home, caught it on the news."

"Madness, man," Aaron said softly. "Street was packed, nothin' but black on black, and all this blue comin' down. Some of the young bloods, man—hotheads—was stoppin' cars, pullin' folk out." He paused and slowly shook his head. "White mostly, 'ceptin' one."

Although no one had died, all of the victims had been beaten. Some badly. The news said that one young man (identity withheld) was in a coma and near death. I stared at my friend.

He ignored me and continued to speak, mumbling, avoiding my eyes. "There was one dude. They threw 'im on the ground, whupped 'im like a dog. He curled up like a baby, and they was kickin' 'im. He was beggin' and they was still kickin' 'im. Cavin' 'im in, too. Eff'd 'im up good." He paused and took a long breath. "It was wrong, man."

"What'd you do?" I asked.

"Nothin'. Not a damn thing," he said, his voice a near whisper. "There was too many, man. Even my partners—Marcus 'n them—jumped in. Madness. Then when the cops come, they back off and split. Then the dude gets on his hands and knees— I don' know how—and he look dead at me. I knew 'im, Buddy. Damn, I knew 'im from school. Chinaman named Ron."

"Damn," I said quietly.

"Caught up wit' Marcus the next day. Act like nothin's wrong. Then I ask 'im why he beat that boy, and he jus' shrug and say, 'That punk Chink? Ain' one o' us. No big deal.'"

Stunned, I just looked at the ground, losing myself in a world of small, circular patterns drawn by my finger, hoping that the words I'd heard, I hadn't. In our neighborhood, blacks and Filipinos had shared a bond formed by poverty and bad attitude. We'd always run together—a natural match, or so I'd assumed. Reflexively, I touched the corners of my eyes and traced the contours. Chinese, no doubt, as was my pale (for a Filipino) complexion. "Damn," I repeated. Just who was now "us"? Had I been expelled? Were my traits now targets—entries stamped on a passport to a beating? Or worse?

Aaron continued quietly. "Marcus don' even flinch, man, don' even worry. He say the revolution's on, and that killin' that boy's no big deal."

"He's dead?" News reports hadn't confirmed his death.

Aaron looked at me. "Man," he said quietly, "Jesus couldn' rise from that whuppin'."

Suddenly I was trying to sort through thoughts now jumbled. Was it anger? fear? I looked up at Aaron, studying a face I knew well, and saw colors—blacks and browns—discordant for the first time. I couldn't breathe right. A friend, or was he? I didn't know. "So what you' sayin'," I finally said, "is that stuff's changin' . . ."

Aaron shrugged. "Guess so." Maddening nonchalance! Anger took hold and sweltered. "Like I was sayin', man," I said, slowly at first, and pausing to load each word to follow, deadly and primed, to take aim and squeeze, smoothly, not jerked, to hit the heart of a friendship on a hot August night. "Like I was sayin', some ignorant blood, like that fool Marcus, your friend, he's gonna take me out and it's cool 'cause the fuckin' revolution's on and I ain' black, and it's payback for oppression I had nothin' to do with!" Suddenly I was screaming, almost spitting the words. Inside my head, unseen mallets beat a rhythm, pounding on walls. I glared at Aaron. "Answer me, man," I demanded.

"You didn' ask no question," he said calmly, and turned away.
My eyes tightened, becoming slits—furrowed and focused, the
not-quite-human gateway to a heart filling with rage. The mallets slammed louder, faster. I exploded. "Nigger!" I hissed, using that word for the first time. Surprised, I wondered at the
power of the word. Had I gone too far? But on that night, with
the August heat still thick, anger was my weapon, there to be
used. Again. "You go to college" (aim and squeeze), I said coldly,
"you still just a nigger" (smoothly, not jerked).

Fight or flight, either one, I was ready for both, but not his
reply.

"It's nigga," he scolded as he turned toward me. "Listen to
yo'sef talk, man," he said evenly. "Can' even say it right. You
soun' like a damn white man."

Sound like a white man?

This time I turned away, stunned, only to turn back to the
sound of receding footfalls through the tall grass. Aaron was
walking up the narrow trail that led to and away from this special place. He stopped in a cluster of evergreens. There, at that
remote edge, he became a silhouette that turned to face the water, to face me.

"I'da backed you, man," the silhouette said, its words sounding like the first notes of a dirge. "Come down to it, I'da backed
you, my brother. Against Marcus. Against anyone."

The silhouette paused before speaking again. "Brother mine."
It spoke slowly, sadly. Then slower, sadder: "Brother no more."
I wanted to call out but held back, knowing I was too late. Aaron
was gone.

Among evergreens, darkness drops suddenly, like a door

shutting. I sat by the lagoon for a long time, staring at nothing, my focus broken only by the sound of an unseen splash—a fish, bass I guessed, leaping from the water. It seemed to hang in the air before its loud, returning slap signalled reentry. A leaping, hungry fish, normally a good omen, but not that night. I whispered a curse and began to walk up the trail and away.

There'd be no shelter; not even here.

Home

Vietnam hunted Rico over time, leaving marks of its pursuit—a piece of flesh here, a hole in his soul there. It started in 1968, just after the generals dropped acid, entered a trance, and spoke of lights shining at the ends of tunnels— a hallucination quickly snuffed by the fury of Tet. Rico was there, running for cover in the rubble of a city called Hue. Somehow he survived the carnage, the bodies piled upon bodies piled upon lies.

He even survived the rest of his tour, and resurfaced in Seattle, our hometown. He called, and one dreary morning, we sat over coffee in an old, smoky cafe near the University of Washington.

He was tired—thick, dark stubble and bloodshot eyes—but that was nothing new. I'd seen him in worse shape during the day, and wearing the same clothes he'd worn two midnights before. "Partied too hearty," he'd mumble. "Too good, too sweet, too hard to quit. So I didn't." As I studied him I figured that, back in his old haunts, he'd reverted to form.

Despite his haggard appearance, he sounded fine. He just wanted to talk. At the start we tried to pick up where we'd once left it: girls, music, cars, the old neighborhood (still poor, still rowdy). He smiled. Topics raised, discussed—loud, easy teenage laughs from a big trunk of memories—and quickly discarded, pushing us too soon from our common past.

As kids we were best friends, inseparable compadres, promising to be there whenever and forever—from weddings to funerals and all points in between. "Say in your life you fuck up," Rico told me when I was thirteen. "You know, everyone hates you and you die. I'll bring you home, man, dig your hole, say a prayer, and burn some incense. You know, I'll purify your butt. Then stick you in the ground." He paused. "You can do the same for me."

I nodded. It was an odd thought from someone so young, but strangely comforting. Vietnam changed it all.

I was in first year, I said, here at the UW. He shrugged. "I know, Buddy. Maybe I'll join you."

Sure. The truth was Rico hated school, and the teachers hated him. He was a hard dude, project-raised by his Indian mother, his Filipino father having left for an evening stroll to Chinatown without bothering to return. At Franklin High, the teachers dogged him—too much pomade, too much attitude—and counted the days until graduation or expulsion, whichever came first. For guys like Rico, college was out of the question; their counselors kept telling them so. Two choices, they said: the military or jail.

I knew he still hated school, whatever the level. He was just talking to make me feel at ease, like we still had something in common. His hope, mine too, but neither of us was sure.

"Maybe I'll join you," he said again, each word a piece of cork, to plug gaps between his first day in Vietnam and now. For a guy not yet twenty, he'd already seen and suffered a life's worth.

I wasn't sure if he'd talk about the war, wasn't sure if I wanted him to. For now, Rico just stared at his coffee mug, lost in a distant, foreign zone I was happy not to know. "Hey, man," I said, trying not to sound worried. "Majestics be playin' down at Parker's. Got horns, plenty ladies. I know you got the moves. Gotta have them moves. You still the man, Rico. You still the . . ."

"Damn, Buddy, this is what kept me goin'," was all he said, still staring at the large mug, squeezing it with both hands. "Just sittin' here, you know, drinkin' coffee, kickin' back 'n bullshittin'. Just when I'd lose it, or think I would, I knew I'd come back here. And now I'm here and . . . don't know how to act." He paused. "Hated it, man," he finally said. "Bullshit. Figured that out quick, the whole fuckin' war. Used to think maybe somethin' good 'd come outa this. That's what I used to tell m'self. But that's bullshit, too. Maybe someday LBJ come check out the crib and say, 'Sorry for the bullshit, Corporal Divina.' And I say, 'What took you so long, you pasty big-eared cowboy motherfucker?'"

He then started to laugh, quietly at first, but the sound rose swiftly to its apex—a loud table-pounding bug-eyed crescendo, full of rage and unseen wounds. I glanced at the floor, unsure of what to say. But I had to say something. "Rico," I said softly. "Remember me? I ain't the enemy."

That seemed to calm him. He stared at me for a moment—blinking, trying to identify my face—before slumping in his chair like an old fighter, badly overmatched and beaten beyond sport. "Sorry, man," he mumbled. "Shit was way outa line. Sorry."

"Cool," I said, as I grabbed both cups, now empty. A diversion—I needed one, we both did. What could I say next? I rose quickly and headed toward the self-service refill stand, making sure I took my time. "Sugar?" I asked loudly, knowing full well the recipe: two lumps, well stirred, no cream.

He held up two fingers.

I could only stir so long and started to walk back, still no idea what to say, but hoping for the best.

Rico let me slide. "It was hard," he said evenly as I settled in my chair. I recognized the somber tone and knew he saved it only for serious matters. But almost two years had passed, and I wasn't so sure anymore. I looked at him, studying the lines and contours of a face I knew as well as my own. Looking for hints— a twitch, some giveaway. He was clean, no trace of that wild, unforgiving look that struck fear in childhood enemies. I figured it was gone, not likely to reappear, at least not today. I relaxed.

"The hardest part was comin' down here," he continued, as he rolled his eyes toward tables full of young folks with long hair. A few were sneaking hostile glances at this young old man who didn't fit. "Shoulda seen the looks when I strolled in," he said.

"You ain't been back long enough," I said. "That, plus your fatigues, your haircut, and that damn Marine bulldog you got painted on your arm. Man, you hard to miss."

I started to chuckle, but stopped when I looked at Rico. He didn't hear me. "I did some foul shit," he said in a monotone. "Stuff I ain't proud of. Like one time, we got hit hard, lotsa guys down. Lost friends, ace buddies. Then we found 'im, this one VC." He paused, his breath labored, his face flushed. A thin film of perspiration started to form on his upper lip and forehead. I didn't want to hear this; it rode him too hard.

"Rico . . ."

He ignored me and continued in his monotone. "Three of us dogged 'im, man. Dude was wounded—a big hole in his shoulder—and we hurt 'im some more. By the time we was done, he was beggin' to die. Didn't understand a word, but I knew the look."

"Rico," I said, this time more forcefully. I gestured wildly with my hands. He ignored me.

"Took parts, man. Stripped 'm like a Chevy, startin' with the ears . . ."

I slumped suddenly in my chair, massaging my temples, trying hard to make the grisly image disappear. If he noticed my reaction, he didn't show it. There was no emotion, not even the slightest trace of pain or remorse.

"But they got no right to judge me," he continued. "They ain't got no right. I was there doin' it for them—with their safe little smug-assed lives and their daddies' accounts—doin' fucked-up things, livin' like some hunted animal. And they got the nerve to give me these looks, like I'm a criminal. But least no one's said nothin', least not yet, least not to my face . . ."

I wondered as I listened—each bitter word corroding our bond—do I still know him? Do I stay or leave? For a moment I wasn't sure, as I tried to reconcile the present and the past. Recollection brought resolve as I remembered childhood scenes and lessons learned. In our world, friendship meant loyalty, simple as that. Whatever happened in Vietnam, Rico was still my friend.

"Rico," I said sharply, grabbing his sleeve. The move surprised him.

"Huh?" he said, as he yanked his arm back.

"You out now, man," I whispered, "outta the jungle."

He stared at me and blinked. For a moment, his eyes showed no sign of recognition. Finally, he sighed. "Maybe not, man," he said softly. "Been thinkin', and I figured it out. Growin' up like we did, we was screwed. 'Ceptin' I took it one step further and screwed myself. Now I'm bringin' it home."

I nodded. He sipped coffee.

"Coulda died there," he said with a shrug. "Maybe shoulda,

but so what? Wouldn't a mattered no damn way." He took another sip. He said that, by coming home, he'd come to grasp a
disturbing truth: in this, his hometown, none of it would've mattered. He felt that no one—except his family, me, and a few
other friends—would have cared, or cried, or even known his
name.

"Just like before," he shrugged. "Ain't nothin' changed."

"But you can change it," I said. "Man, with GI, you got college."

"You got college," he said bitterly. His tone surprised me.
"Killers don't go to college," he said, as he drifted back to the
zone. "Greg, John, Henry . . ." He was speaking softly now, rev-
erently, almost whispering this litany of names that I knew by
heart. They were young Filipinos, like Rico and me, draftees
from a poor neighborhood that the war hit hard. Most made it
back from Vietnam; a few didn't. Like Rico, they went to public
high schools—vocational class, their counselors told them, since
you got no future anyway. For those who didn't go to college, voc
class was a holding pen on the road to the draft.

Me? I was lucky. My mom had a dream. She was an immigrant from the Philippines and didn't know better. College, she
said to us kids. College, she told us, to avoid your father's blood-
money life of cannery and field. That meant Catholic schools,
but she was willing to pay the price—scrub floors, cut hair, whatever.

So she did, and in high school I found myself learning from
the feared Christian Brothers: big, rough Irishmen whose vows
of celibacy soured further their bad dispositions. Still, it was a
minor flaw, because in the end I had choices, something Rico
never had.

". . . Teddy, Norman, Vic, Eddie," he droned. "Shit," he said. "Eddie didn't make it."

"I know," I said solemnly.

"Check it out, man," he said. "Saw Teddy there in Saigon. Eddie, too. Remember Eddie? Big-lipped fat-head can't-walk-without-trippin' Eddie?" I nodded as Rico recalled the memory of our homely, awkward friend. "Teddy says he gonna help 'im out, throw down some coin if he got to. Eddie's first taste." Rico smiled, then stared at me. "Then a week later, Eddie's gone. Boy never had no kinda luck. Probably messed up in Saigon, too, 'n died a virgin." He sipped from his coffee. "Damn," he sighed. "A fuckin' virgin, man," he whispered. "Died a teenage, fuckin' virgin."

As Rico slowly shook his head, I sat silent, edgy, without a reply. He'd have to finish, and I'd just have to ride it wherever it was going.

"Man, seein' 'em all in Saigon, what's the chances? Just like home. Everyone's there." He chuckled, hollow and joyless, then looked at me, his gaze burning through the present to recall too soon each detail of the past. " 'Ceptin' you, Buddy," he said quietly. " 'Ceptin' you."

I shivered. His accusation demanded my response. He was testing me—like he'd tested others—and in the process, had crossed a line we both knew from childhood. Friend or not, I had to come back. Hard.

"Rico," I said calmly, "we'll talk about it, but not here. You got shit to say, say it there." I nodded toward the door. I rose quickly and turned to walk away. Rico just stared. He said nothing and made no move to follow.

Once outside I waited, a bit nervous, hoping he wouldn't show.

There was a gulf between us, that much was clear. But old friendships die hard, and he was still my friend. After a few minutes I glanced at my watch. Ten minutes till class. I started walking toward campus, knowing that if I hustled, I could still make it.

This was my first year of college. Mom's dream, mine too. I didn't want to be late.

It was easy to get lost at the UW, with its spacious and beautiful evergreen campus—prettier than the picture on its brochure—its crowded classes and arrogant, impersonal professors. It was easy to forget a troubled friendship, to ignore the devils that chased Rico while I chased a dream. But even then, buried as I was in books and papers, I'd surface to pause and think, and mourn a wounded bond. I promised myself I'd call, make the first move to reconcile, but later, after this midterm, this report, this final. I never made that call, didn't have to.

One evening near the end of spring term, Rico just showed up at my dorm. He was clean shaven and neatly dressed; a long-sleeved shirt hid the bulldog on his arm. "Thought I'd visit," was all he said, with a sheepish what-can-I-say grin. It was all he needed. I dropped my books and we talked through the night.

Rico claimed he was better now, that each new day meant another one away from hell. He figured it was progress. To help speed the process, he'd done the unthinkable by enrolling in school, a junior college, where, for the first time, he was taking his studies seriously. He had no idea where he was going, but he wasn't in a rush. His GI Bill covered tuition plus provided a stipend, not much, but enough to buy more time away from hell. At the end we parted friends, not like before, but better than in the recent past. At least it was a start.

Over the next few weeks, we saw each other a couple more times, more in passing—a quick cup of coffee, lunch on the run—than anything else. We were both buried in finals, but we agreed to meet when they were over and hang out, just like the old days.

When exams ended, Rico was gone. I called his mom's house. No luck. He'd left two weeks earlier. No warning, and no word to anyone of his destination, if there was one. She said she'd call me if she heard. I sighed when I hung up the phone. Vietnam was still too close; the devils, I figured, were closing in.

I didn't hear from Rico until September, when I received a card postmarked Boston. "Had to leave, Buddy," Rico wrote. "Explain later."

He never did explain. The best I got were postcards with no return address, care of my mom's house. Ours was a cryptic one-way correspondence, a few scrawled lines proving he was still alive.

The next card was from Missoula. Urban/rural, I figured, he's comparing the two, looking where to settle. Then came several from big cities—from LA, New York, and Chicago—followed by two from postmarked dots on the map—Dickinson, North Dakota, and Marysville, California. I kept all his cards in a shoebox, all arranged in chronological order.

On my wall hung a map of the US on which I marked and dated each city and burg, straight red lines joining one to another. At the start, I wondered: Did he have a geographic preference? Was there a pattern? The jumble of lines said no. Rico was running. I wondered when he'd stop.

Maybe he already had.

After Marysville, the cards stopped coming. As months of

silence turned into one, then two years, I didn't know if Rico was well, or even alive. I called his house. "Gone," his mother said. "Just like his dad. Your guess's good as mine."

Even Kitty, his favorite sister, couldn't help. No word, she shrugged.

There was nothing to do but wait and hope that somehow he was still on the move, that the devils hadn't won. They hadn't, at least not as of September 1973, when I finally received a card. Judging from the postmark, Rico was in Santa Fe. Unlike his previous brief messages, this one was expansive—three full paragraphs. He apologized for his silence, but explained he'd found a woman. He was thinking of bringing her home, having her meet family and friends. Marriage was next, he said, and would I be his best man? Of course, I thought, but had no way to convey my acceptance. Just like the other cards, this one had no return address.

As always, I'd just have to wait. Still, this was good news, the best in years, but it had a shelf life of one month. In October Rico wrote again, this time from Miami. "Messed up," he said. "Keep trying till I get it right."

Miami's was the last one, not just for 1973, but for several more years. It was a period during which I'd managed to graduate from law school, marry and divorce, and enter and leave the law and some other professions. Throughout this time there was no word from Rico. And frankly, I'd stopped thinking about him, except for those rare occasions when I'd see Kitty or another family member.

When I'd ask about her brother, Kitty would just shrug. Same with the others. No word, same as before. I sensed Kitty was getting tired of the question; the last time I saw her, I didn't even ask.

Even if he were still alive, Rico had died to those he'd left behind. I'd moved on. My memory of him had slipped to the point that I was starting to forget details of the events we'd shared, details I had once recalled with precision and fondness. Now, each time I replayed the tape, they changed. I knew that over time they'd change again. And again. I'd start forgetting words, actions, emotions that had once made our friendship strong.

Rico stayed dead until a drizzly September afternoon in 1988, more than nineteen years after he'd left town. I was sitting alone in my apartment, listening to the rain and the drone of a baritone radio voice. I'd been thinking about him, maybe because I was nearing a midpoint of sorts, my thirty-eighth year, a melancholy mark on the line somewhere between hope and the grave. As kids, we used to celebrate birthdays, his and mine, with great abandon, trying to squeeze in every second of those magic twenty-four hours. And now, between marriages, and near the end of another unsatisfactory career (teaching math to ninth graders who refused to compute, refused to learn, didn't want to; not even Mom could've changed their minds, I told myself), I suddenly wished Rico was here, just hanging out.

Two days later, on the day of my birth, I dropped by my parents' place. Mom always treated my birthdays much more seriously than I did. She hugged me and gave me the rundown on the invitees, including immediate family (father, brother, and sister) plus a list of shirt-tail relations that grew with each passing year. After parading me in front these new and vaguely remembered faces, she whispered in my ear. "You got a card on the kitchen table," she said. "It's from Rico, but I thought he was dead."

At first I was silent, too stunned to reply. "He was," I finally said.

I rushed to the kitchen to see an oversize postcard featuring the garish lights of Reno at night. Quickly I flipped it over, skipped the message, and started at the end. Rico's initials. No doubt.

Then the beginning. He said he was wishing me happy birthday, seeing as how he'd overlooked a few. It was almost twenty years since he'd left; he needed to come home. He was missing friends and family plus more—the mountain skyline, clear rivers and lakes, the beauty of the place. I knew what he meant. Because of that beauty, folks from here tolerate the rain, an eight-month squall. They don't wander much, and if they do, the direction's circular.

It was Rico's time to come home.

And his card lifted the pall on this, the first day of my thirty-eighth year. I even managed to enjoy the party despite the crush of strangers and the too-personal inquiries Filipinos so dearly love. Sample Question: "Where's your beautiful wife?" Sample Answer: "She left me."

At the end, I took his card with me back to my apartment. Somewhere in my closet was an old shoebox. Tonight it would house a new tenant. I hoped it would be the last.

The rest of 1988 passed without a word; by year's end, I'd given up hope. Then in January, Kitty called. Rico was dead, killed in a flophouse fire in Stockton, California. (Stockton? Our immigrant fathers were there in the thirties and forties, bent low over asparagus rows, some dropping from the heat. Slave wages, slave lives. They got smart and left, but Rico returned.)

Kitty wasn't sure of the details, just what the coroner had told her. He was almost a John Doe, his body burned so bad it took a while to find out who he was. His family was planning to ship what was left home to Seattle, for burial. She wanted to know if I'd be there for the funeral. Nothing fancy, she said, just family and a few friends.

I said I would.

Rico would be buried in a cemetery atop Capitol Hill. It was an especially lovely spot, quiet and still, from which could be seen mountains on two sides, and closer, deep-blue lakes that almost touched the base of the hill. On the morning of the burial, I walked with Kitty to the grave. There, an old priest, possibly bothered by the cold, rushed through the prayers. It seemed we'd just arrived, and suddenly the ceremony was over. It was an odd, indifferent end. I looked at Kitty who pulled me toward her.

"Rico left you something," she whispered. "Before he died, he gave a lady friend a box of stuff for each of us. She called and said that he'd given it to her the week before the fire. Made her promise she'd send it if anything happened. Got it yesterday." Kitty handed me a small box wrapped in newspaper, smaller than a fist. My first name was in the right-hand corner.

"Damn," I said softly, and put it in my coat pocket.

Kitty and I walked toward the gate, where we parted. She joined her family, while I headed toward my car. As I drove away, I wondered about the box. What did it contain? What message from the dead? Did I even want to find out? I sighed. Decisions could wait on a cup of coffee, which on this morning had to be strong and black, no cream or sugar. I drove toward the UW and the nearby coffee shop where, on a cold, cloudy morning much like this, Rico and I had once sat.

Between sips of black coffee and puffs of smoke, I stared at the small packet that lay on the table before me. I couldn't imagine its contents, not even after a third cup and the near exhaustion of my pack of Marlboros. Apprehension had checked curiosity to create gridlock. After several hours, the packet was still sealed. This couldn't go on. Whatever it was, it was also my friend's last word. I owed it to Rico to open it—but at the cemetery, not here.

As I walked slowly toward Rico's grave, I started to shake, but not from the cold. I slowed but didn't stop, because I knew if I did, I wouldn't continue. "Dammit!" I shouted; I hoped that a noise so fierce and focused would purge my fear, or at least suppress it enough to keep me moving. It must have worked. I soon found myself at Rico's freshly filled grave.

I set the packet on his headstone and unsealed it quickly before I could change my mind. A small box. I opened it—a folded note and a medal, a Silver Star resting on a tiny cardboard bed. I stared at the medal; Rico'd never mentioned courage. I then grabbed the note and walked to the base of a nearby pine: "Since you're reading this, guess I didn't make it home. Least some stuff did, part of which I'm proud of. Take care of it."

I exhaled. Not too bad, nothing too eerie. Just two items. I'd fold up the note, take it to my place, and put it in the shoebox. Maybe the same for the Silver Star. Simple. I returned to the grave to pick up the medal.

As my fingers nudged the cardboard, it gave way. There was more at the bottom of the box. I removed the cardboard to find a flat, tiny bundle, about the size of a dime, wrapped in gauze, which I quickly peeled back. I gasped as my fingers touched a black piece of something shriveled, drained, and pressed. It might have been flesh, maybe part of an earlobe.

I dropped the bundle and stepped away from the grave, curses trumpeting my retreat. I stopped, lit up a smoke, and nervously started to circle the bundle, first left to right, then reverse. I had no idea what Rico wanted or what I should do next.

I might be circling still, but for a loose piece of sod on a fresh grave adjacent to Rico's. My right foot rode it as it quickly gave way. I tried to steady myself but realized it was too late. My unplanned momentum was too fast. So I relaxed to prevent injury, and just accepted the fall. When I landed, I was eye level with the hated bundle, maybe two feet away.

As I lay there, I started to laugh—it was hard not to—and fished for a smoke. I slowly sat up and lit my last cigarette. The slapstick tumble, which had ruined my slacks and removed my dignity, had also stolen my fear. I just sat there, trying to focus through tiny swirls of smoke on what Rico wanted.

Bring him home, I thought. But how? I scanned the years of our friendship, especially our time as kids. I started to recall with unusual clarity a conversation in which he'd promised to bury me. It was an odd thought then, less so now. I'd promised the same.

I rose and walked to Rico's grave, where I picked up the medal and placed it on the headstone. It belonged here and nowhere else; he'd earned it. Next, I put the note and the tiny bundle back inside the cardboard box, which I then lay on his grave.

"Fire to purify," I said, and I lit the box's four corners before stepping back to watch the small flame flare toward a darkening afternoon sky. The fire rose and fell, leaving embers, then ashes, then nothing more.

It was dusk when I started to walk slowly toward the entrance. Outside the gate, a street light's glare and the sounds of cars signaled that life moved on. I would join it soon, and gladly, but not before turning one last time in the direction of Rico's grave. In the distance, the running lights of small boats shimmered on the lake, and beyond, the jagged white tips of the Cascade silhouette lingered against the onset of night. A gift for the senses; a gift to my friend. Reason enough to come home.

A Life Well Lived

Chris had his flaws, like the stench of dried, cheap wine and stale cigarettes which clung to a visitor's clothing, threatening to seep under the skin. It never seemed to leave and defied soap and water, fresh air, even the passing of time. I can smell it still.

The main room of his Chinatown apartment was small and cluttered. As always, he sat on a chair on the far side by the window, facing the door. From that spot, he rarely moved.

There was an adjoining bedroom, which I never saw him use. Years ago, he'd lost a leg in an accident. I wondered if the effort to transfer from one room to the other was sometimes too much, and he'd spend the night in the chair. He was sitting there when I first visited him in 1972.

"Hello, Manong Chris," I said.

His last name was Mensalvas, and I'd met him only once before, when I was a child. On that occasion, my mother had told me that he was a Communist, but she'd added that he was also a nice man. Dad agreed. And for them both—the most non-ideological of souls—the latter trait was far more important than political beliefs.

They were right; I sensed that immediately as I introduced myself to him all these years later. He smiled as I walked over to shake his hand. He liked my father, he said, and knew him from the cannery days. And yes, he'd heard about the proposed suit against King County and would gladly be a plaintiff.

We talked a bit more, but mostly I just listened and watched. He was a small man and seemed, with an empty pants leg dangling, even smaller. His white hair was combed back, gangster style, in a fashion common decades earlier. But the pomade was gone, not needed—his hair curved backward without it, a victim of persistent training.

He was well over sixty, with a face that was still smooth, golden brown. His eyes slanted slightly. When he laughed, which was often, they'd sometimes disappear.

After an hour or so I left, promising to return with more information about the impending action. He'd be a plaintiff suing King County in a class action on behalf of his fellow residents in Chinatown. The suit was an attempt to stop construction of the domed stadium, the Kingdome, which was to be built nearby. Many feared that the rise in surrounding property values would close Chinatown's low-income residential hotels.

In 1972 I was a first-year law student serving as a liaison between the legal team and the Chinatown residents. I was twenty-one years old. As things turned out, we eventually lost, and if I'd been older, the loss wouldn't have surprised me. It was, after all, the dissent of a handful of poor, aging Filipinos against the power of King County. It was hardly a fair fight.

I suspect that's why Chris laughed. He'd never been in a fair fight. And compared with what he'd faced in earlier years—the beatings, jailings, attempted deportations—this bout with the county was a summer picnic.

At his age, what mattered most was the chance to joust, whatever the outcome. He could've told me we were going to lose, but he didn't. And besides, he enjoyed the attention.

But, to get back to the preliminaries, when I returned a couple of days later, Chris was no longer alone. Sitting with him was another old Filipino, similar in size and complexion but unnaturally stiff and upright. Chris was holding a tiny shot glass gently to his friend's lips; the man sipped a drop of the whiskey but couldn't move his head to gulp down the remainder. Chris was patient, almost maternal, as he coaxed his friend.

"Hello," Chris greeted me as I eased into a chair opposite both of them. "This is Mat Lagunilla, a friend of mine. He's had a stroke."

Mat was in bad shape, that much was obvious. He was almost immobile, unable to speak.

"Mat," Chris said cheerfully, "will also join the suit. Won't you, Mat?"

With great effort, Lagunilla nodded slightly in apparent agreement.

This time I'd brought certain legal papers, among them authorization forms that permitted the attorneys to sue on behalf of the signatories. I handed one to Chris. He looked at it, read it slowly, and gave the first one to Mat. Chris also gave him a pen, and a book upon which he placed the form.

"Sign it, Mat," Chris said. He did, and to this day, I don't know how. He was half dead, or at least not quite alive. And he held that pen crudely, like a child with a crayola learning to write. Yet, somehow, he retained enough of himself to stab, scrawl, and scribble his name onto that piece of paper.

Chris later told me that Mat had returned to the Philippines, and I knew what he meant. "Returned" was a euphemism that had little to do with returning and everything to do with dying. As so many had done before him, Mat returned home to die. In a sense, his ravaged condition was a disguised blessing. Death was quick. He didn't have to explain his poverty and apparent failures to relatives anxious to know of the world he'd left. After

Mat had finally and mercifully died, Chris showed me a snap-shot of the funeral. In the middle lay old Mat in repose, like one of those statues of saints who always look piously upward.

"This is Mat," Chris said, succinctly and without emotion. "Dead as a doorknob."

It's a Filipino custom to take pictures of the dead. And in my own experience, I've seen more pictures of doorknobs than living relatives. For American tastes, it may be a bit macabre to remember the departed by Polaroid, but no more so than to forget the living. Because, at one point, Chris and Mat were alive but living badly, forgotten by the Community they had helped to build.

The Community was the umbrella organization for all other organizations and served as the official representative for Filipinos in Seattle. Its headquarters were in a former bowling alley on Empire Way, and it resembled, and does to this day, a bowling alley on Empire Way. On Saturday nights, members danced at the bowling alley, and on Sunday evenings, they played bingo. On certain Sunday afternoons—the first one of each month—they held Community Council meetings. Council members were the more prominent fish in a very small pond.

The guests on those special Sunday afternoons were a mixed group, to say the least. A few of them were short, comical creatures who, like hamsters, scurried between tables. Their most fervent Sunday wish was to prevent gossip from including their names. Many were not so insecure, or if they were, did not display it publicly on the Lord's day. And some were good, even admirable, people.

There were those, however, who were neither admirable, nor insignificant, nor harmlessly silly. They were hard and powerful men who made their living by being harder and more powerful than those whom they robbed. They were Union officials, and, in those days, a few were particularly notorious for accepting kickbacks from workers dispatched to the Alaskan canneries. On those special Sunday afternoons, they sat, impeccable and polished, with their legs crossed, wearing suits that shone even in the afternoon light.

From the first drop of the gavel until the final pointless speech, they dominated the meetings, exploiting all the elements of the Filipino oratorical style—exaggeration, gesticulation, slander, and perspiration. One, in particular, favored this approach and used it, in equal measure, to praise himself and damn his enemies. Of them all, he was the most sinister, and the most obnoxious.

At that time, his star was high within the Union and the Community. He was pompadoured and slick, and he wore his blue-black mane plastered against the sides of his head. The mixture of grease and hair was so thick no ordinary comb could ever penetrate it, much less navigate it, successfully. It was bullet proof, or appeared so. From the back, his head resembled a dark, medieval turret, strangely out of place in a bowling alley on Empire Way.

Whenever I'd mention Turret Head and the others, Chris would begin a long train of slurred invectives, each more horrendous than the preceding. This train, unlike most trains, pulled out on time, every time. Half drunk, he'd spit those words into the air, stumbling over letters as he raced to throw them all out.

What he said was true. Turret Head and his friends were bad adjectives. But for the old man, their repugnance cut a special slice—painful, razor thin, invisible to most eyes. They were traitors. That's what he really meant. And as traitors, they left no signs of their work—no wounds or blood, just damage.

And what did they betray? His Union, ILWU Local 37, something Chris loved more than a little. If, at one time, he'd been important to the Community, he was double that to his Union. Chris was its parent, teacher, and nag. And over the course of decades, he'd guided, coaxed, and scolded the concept of unionization into the minds of Filipino workers. His friend and countryman, the author Carlos Bulosan, said that Chris Mensalvas was the best Filipino organizer. Bulosan was right.

Chris had seen it all—tentative organizational efforts, an early independent Union, and later, affiliations with powerful internationals. The ILWU—the International Longshoremen's & Warehousemen's Union—was the last of the line.

With the anti-red hysteria after World War II, most of organized labor shied away from Filipino unionists. The Congress of Industrial Organizations (CIO), which had previously claimed the Seattle local, suddenly expelled it in 1949. Into the breach came Harry Bridges and his Longshoremen. It was a militant and tough organization, and Bridges, if he wasn't a Communist, as he subsequently claimed, gave a most persuasive impersonation.

This was a perfect match at an imperfect time. The McCarthy era devastated the Left, and the ensuing years witnessed historic legal and political battles. For Chris and his Union, the times were especially hard, and Local 37 was particularly vulnerable. As aliens, many Filipino members were subject to deportation for "improper" political affiliations.

Yet, somehow, he and the Union survived it all—the harassment, the arrests, and the subsequent court fights. All that remains of that turbulent time are its survivors, their unwritten history, and a list of bitter court cases with innocuous names.

It wasn't as if the Local were red throughout; the ideology of the rank and file was hardly uniform. Some couldn't tell Groucho Marx from Karl, a rather distant cousin. Yet, they stayed loyal to Chris because he understood them and their needs, and he spoke their language.

That was his magic. He could speak to anyone, and that person would believe, or would at least want to believe. Like a mathematician, he always found the common denominator, that rare, slender isthmus of language where the same words spoken, sometimes between strangers, had the same meaning.

Chris's talent—that human touch—worked in spite of his ideology, not because of it. He was an orthodox Communist, a Stalinist. It was a brutal, bankrupt political belief. But that's what he was and, as such, he abhorred the great infidelity—Trotskyism—and had little patience for Social Democracy, Maoism, or other deviations. Still, his friends included Catholics, lapsed and active, plus Maoists, pseudo-Maoists, an occasional Democrat, and a wide array of political agnostics.

With no small pride, he once told me he'd held his card for decades, and that Bulosan was also a long-time Party member. Small wonder, really. In those hard days, only the Communists supported the hopes of Filipino labor.

But that was long ago, and it's hard to explain his enduring loyalty. During the 1950s, he could've renounced his ideology for a much easier life. He could've quit the Union; some of his comrades did, but not Chris, who faced the maelstrom and held firm. I can only suggest that it's the best Filipino trait to never abandon those who gave you shelter. And for my money, Chris Mensalvas was the best of Filipinos.

I can imagine what he was like in the past, because even at his advanced age and stage of deterioration, he could reach you.

He'd glide past the defenses of cynicism and logic that afflict the young—these he'd evade with embarassing ease—and would speak to your heart. It was an uncomfortable conversation, made without the listener's permission, but made nonetheless.

There was one day in particular when this one-legged Merlin was at his best, conjuring with his own words what incantations could never achieve. We were drinking, but not drunk. Suddenly, he started speaking in absurdities—non-sequiturs and gross exaggerations. He was the man of faith, and I, the infidel. His passion took on my logic, and, unfortunately, the latter wasn't home, having been dispatched to guard against a foe that had already passed.

That's a danger of wine with old men. Sometimes, they don't recognize the accepted rules of order or, if they do, it's selective at best. Unlike the young, the old conform the rules to their lives, not the reverse.

So we sat there, his passion and my rules. It was a confrontation of sorts, but hardly a contest.

Chris started innocently enough with a comment that Seattle and its politics were insignificant on any nonlocal scale. I readily agreed. He then added that there were other, far greater struggles elsewhere. He wanted, he said, to go to the Philippines to fight Ferdinand Marcos, the nation's dictator. And he wanted me to take him.

Of course, the proposal was absurd—an old cripple and a boy in the devil's lair. But then I looked at him straight. Chris was serious. I wanted to say yes; the word slid from my mind but lodged in my throat. Instead I couched my reply, with newly acquired skill, in the old legal caveats—"maybe," "perhaps," "possibly."

Chris sensed my hesitation, and he gracefully accepted my

response, what weak response there was. For my sake, he drank some more. The extra alcohol took its normal course, blurring our conversation and consigning his original proposal to oblivion.

Chris, I'm sure, would've been more than happy to die in the Philippines. It was better than rotting in his chair. He'd have died for something he believed in—a consistent end to a consistent life. He called, and I wasn't ready. And to this day, I don't know if much has changed. I returned to my world, a place far safer than the one Chris had proposed to enter. After that, my visits came less frequently, and when they did, he seemed more haggard than the time before.

In 1974 I finally graduated from law school. I invited Chris to the Commencement. Before the ceremony, I stopped by to pick him up. He couldn't make it. "Gout," he said.

He'd been drinking and his good foot hurt too much. It was like that during the last few years. Age, alcohol, and, I think, the onset of despair were finally taking their toll.

There's a misleading vision of the last days of old men: the spry old fighter sitting weary after countless bouts, but courageous, chipper, and coherent until the end. It's a nice image, and sometimes it even happens. But the last days of Chinatown's poor are not often like that.

Chris was an old man, confined to a chair for most of the day, the old drunk smell of wine and nicotine enveloping him. And worse than that, he realized his people had forgotten, or never knew, their common purpose. Even those who should have remembered had chosen to forget whatever it was they once stood for.

He's been dead now for several years, his last breath drawn in a fire in his apartment. He was trapped, I suspect, as much by his condition and his past as by smoke and flame.

Dead as a doorknob.

Ashes to ashes, dust to dust, the cycle continues. Survivors survive, and the dead are soon forgotten. It's an eternal process, as natural as the summer sky. But even in nature, there's loss and sometimes mourning. Yet the fear of death often causes a premature rush from the dead. In pell-mell fashion, we forget too soon the meaning of a life well lived.

Those who knew Chris Mensalvas and have chosen to forget him have perhaps lost the most. And what have they lost? A sense of vision which, for Chris, was greater than himself. The dream was flawed, as was he. But he clutched it, dreamer that he was, from his first day until his last.

In the days of our colonizers, the Philippines was a dangerous place—a land of incessant and futile revolt. Its inhabitants were dangerous because they dreamed dangerous dreams. In Seattle, among his people, that trait has vanished, the victim of a trade-off—a sense of vision bartered away for gratification and comfort. To his credit, it's an exchange the old man never made.

Rest well, Manong Chris.

The Wedding

Uncle Leo had his chances to leave Chinatown. Like marriage. But there were always excuses. "My friends," he'd say, referring to his Chinatown cronies. "I'd have to leave 'em. Can't take 'em with me, you know, and put 'em in the yard." Instead, his friends left him, death or marriage the most common vehicles. A few of the old-timers even married smart—like my dad, Leo's cousin— who returned to the Philippines and married a bright, hardworking, frugal woman, telling her sweet lies about life in wonderland. Wonderland, the America of Filipino dreams, survived the trip over but crumbled on the first night here, in Chinatown in my dad's hot-plate room, not too different or too far from the one Leo still called home. Sleep light, he said, they were leaving early tomorrow—asparagus crew, destination Walla Walla.

Walla Whata? She must have wondered.

But Mom had survived World War II, when her home had been an open grave into which two brothers had fallen. She figured that poverty was easy, and a dream delayed was better than none at all. So she hung in, determined to work and to save what she and my father made. Marriage, as she saw it, meant stable (not migratory) work, double paychecks, a down payment on a small house, escape from Chinatown, and a family.

It would take time. For more than twenty years, my father had moved from field to cannery to field, depending on the season, roaming the West and returning to Seattle only for the winter. He'd even come to like it, this only life he'd known—particularly the Alaskan canning season, where the Union was strong, his friends true, the scenery beautiful, the money decent, and (he never said it, but she knew) the native girls receptive. He'd have to give it all up. And eventually he did, one season at a time. Field work went first. That was easy. Bad pay, hot and hard work. Easy. But summers in Alaska? There Dad drew the line, or tried to.

"Salmon," he'd roar. "It's my life."

"Then live it," she'd calmly reply, "with someone else, like one of your Indians with crazy hair."

The birth of children (my brother and I) slowly made Dad's goodbyes inevitable—to salmon, Alaska, buddies, and dark-brown girls with crazy hair. But his Alaskan sojourns didn't immediately end. There was always one more season (the last, he'd promise), then another, then another, until one summer, when my brother and I were seven and four, he just stayed home. "You boys gettin' too big," was all he said.

Dad eventually settled into a nine-to-five factory job. He adapted to the new routine—year-round marriage, year-round job, fifty-two Sundays plus holy days—surprisingly well and eventually grew to like it, or at least appeared to. For Mom, that was good enough. This conversion—miraculous to his old friends—made him an enthusiastic witness to the new way. To Dad's way of thinking, good news had to be shared. Had to. And Uncle Leo, who persisted in aimlessness, would be the first recipient.

Dad was blunt. "You need to marry," he'd say. "First your hair goes, then your eyes 'n teeth's next. Whatcha gonna do then? Gum the girlies? Don' be no fool. You almost fifty now. Think ahead. This land's too hard for old men."

Leo ignored him on that and every occasion thereafter. If he chose to respond, it was with the stock litany of marriage-related troubles and headaches plus one: selfish youth. "Ah, Vince," he'd say. "Got hair, got teeth, ain' sixty, got eyes to look at the mirror and tell me I'm still a boy."

Leo was smug, at least in the beginning. In the beginning he had energy to burn, more than enough to attend marriages and celebrations, or later, the inevitable christenings and baptisms. And then (where did the time go?) the weddings of the babies whose baptisms he could recall with depressing clarity. Then finally, after he had turned sixty, the funerals of the men with whom he had come to this not-so-new land forty years earlier.

All this while, Leo preferred the company of Chinatown prostitutes (no troubles, no headaches), the latest being a beautiful young *mestiza* (Filipino-Mexican) who sucked Leo and his savings simultaneously, convincing him, with his sharp Chinese features, that her one-year-old African-Filipino-Mexican baby was really his. My parents were concerned. They warned Leo, but he was stubborn. My father had given up. "Hell with 'im," he said. "Young fool, old fool. He don' change."

So one day Leo took his case to my mother, brandishing a picture pulled from his wallet of this most dissimilar child, a dark and pretty little girl. This, he said, proved his blood tie.

"Don' she look like me?" Leo asked proudly.

Pictures, they say, don't lie. But this one did, or at least it said something to the old man that it said to no one else. My mother studied the photo. "Ah, Leo," she sighed. Finally she replied. "She got two ears, just like you."

Leo also sighed. On this point, a draw. He remained adamant; the child was his, all physical evidence notwithstanding.

Worse, he had started to compound his delusion. He took me aside.

"She loves me, Buddy," he whispered.

"Who?"

"Anita."

"Who's Anita?"

"You know," Leo said with a smile. "Baby's mom."

I wanted to shake him, to tell him that, to this predatory young woman, he was nothing more than a food source, a lonely old man, and a sixty-year-old fool. In that order; nothing more. I looked at Uncle Leo; he was still smiling, probably at the thought of dear Anita. I should have told him; should have, didn't.

"How do you know?" I asked weakly.

"Buddy," he said softly. "She said so."

What could I say? Mom always claimed that, in this country, when Pinoys got old, they got crazy. Maybe it's the cold. Who knows? Look at Leo. Yet, for the sake of family harmony (and Leo's feelings), we just let the matter drop. His romance would have to run its course.

The end came on a dreary Sunday afternoon when Leo returned early from a rained-out day at the fishing piers and found Anita and her pimp going through his room. He didn't have much. His one item of monetary value—a small collection of silver dollars—he kept in an old box, now snug under Anita's arm. Leo called me soon after the incident. He sounded crushed, embarrassed.

"What did you do?" I asked.

"Nothin'."

"Nothing?" I couldn't imagine "nothing." No protest? no curse? no knife in her neck? no . . .

"Nothin'," he repeated evenly. "Jus' let 'em leave."

"Damn, Uncle Leo," I said quietly.

Leo continued. "Wha' can I say? There's nothin' to do."

I was almost speechless. A whispered "fuckin' ho," the best I could muster.

Silence for a few moments, then Leo spoke again. "Buddy," he said slowly. "Gonna leave town for a few days, mebbe go to California. Got a cousin there, ain' seen for twenny years, mebbe more. Don' hear from me for a while, don' worry, okay?"

"Sure," I said. "No problem."

"Jus' one thing," he continued. "Your parents, I know 'em. I know wha' they say, wha' they think . . ."

"Don't worry, Uncle Leo. Your secret's safe," I assured the old man. "I won't tell 'em."

Days turned into weeks, then a month, then two—no word from Uncle Leo. I was starting to worry. My parents were, too. Dad said he'd checked his hotel; Leo was gone, but he'd paid three months in advance. The old Chinese desk clerk didn't know where he was. No word there, either. California maybe? Don't know; maybe the moon.

My folks knew I was close to Leo, that he told me things he'd never tell them. They'd probe and push, but I wouldn't budge. To their inquiries, I'd just shrug: who knows, maybe the moon? Still, two months was a long time to go without word. Then, finally, a phone call—Uncle Leo was home! I'd be there, I promised, within the hour, maybe sooner.

In twenty years, the old metal chair upon which I was sitting had moved maybe twice, its latest position being next to the only window in a tiny walk-up Chinatown room overlooking the corner of 6th and King. But to Uncle Leo, my favorite among what were once so many bachelor uncles, this was home. The old man had lived here his whole twenty years in Seattle, working long hours for short pay at nowhere jobs. Uncle Leo was poor but never cheap, at least not with me. Over time, he'd been the source of candy bars (Hershey's plain), a small treasury of fishing rods, baseball mitts, and, as I got older, sports jackets and fancy wool overcoats. "Ain' got no boy," he'd say. "Guess you'll do. Our secret, so don' tell your folks."

"I need to see you," Leo had said when he called. That was an odd choice of words, Uncle Leo needing anything, especially from me, his lifelong beneficiary. It was his point of honor, grounded in poverty and a deep Filipino sense of pride, never to need, even from those he loved. But now he did, maybe.

When I arrived, he was sitting on the edge of his bed, his attention focused (as it usually was) on a television perched on the dresser. But something was different. This was a new, expensive Japanese model—color—replacing the old black and white, which, after years of faithful service, had finally died.

"It's yours, Buddy," he said without looking up.

I wasn't sure what he meant.

"Jus' don' tell 'em, okay?"

"Tell 'em what, Uncle Leo?"

He finally looked up. "Ah Buddy," he sighed. "Sometimes I wonner you unnerstan' English. You born here, but sometimes I wonner . . ."

"Uncle Leo . . ."

"That," he said calmly, pointing to the new television set. "It's yours."

I was stunned. "But Uncle Leo," I stammered. "I can't take that. You're retired. It's new."

Leo stared at me. "Wha' you mean?" he asked indignantly.

"All this time you only get old stuff from me? Never new? Cost poor Leo too much? Jus' 'cause I live here?" He turned, and with a dramatic sweep, gestured at each of the walls. I followed his hand around the room, noting for the first time the detailed pattern of the faded wallpaper. It was a pastoral scene, complete with depictions of docile farm animals, blonde and bland farm folk, and live roaches who strolled casually between the cracks in the faded green upper pasture and the black top of the guernsey's head. Aside from the insects, I thought the pattern more fitting for a well-appointed child's room than a Chinatown dive.

"Damn landlord," I muttered. "Asshole must've bought it in a sale."

"Wha'?"

"Nothing, Uncle Leo."

Leo went back to watching tv. He was sulking, lonely, full of wounds. Poverty hurt the old man, but pity killed him. What must have hurt worse was the realization, slow to arrive, that the deeper cuts were self-inflicted. In over forty years in the new land, he'd never made it, and now he had nothing to show—no house, no kids, no fortune.

"Where'd you go?" I finally asked.

"Home," he mumbled.

I was puzzled. His home was here—at least for the twenty years I'd known him. Then I remembered that before he came to Seattle, he'd lived a while in Stockton. "California?" I asked.

"No," he said quietly. "Back home. You know, back home." He paused. I was still confused. "Talisay," he whispered.

"The Philippines?" I was stunned. He hated the place, at least that's what he'd said when he returned from a visit five years ago, his first since coming to the States. Too hot, too poor, no running water or toilet paper. His visa was good for two months; he lasted two weeks and swore he'd never return.

"But Uncle Leo," I said. "I thought you couldn't stand . . ." He interrupted me. "Things change," he said calmly.

"Why?"

He shrugged. "Why not?" He reached in his pocket, pulled out a cigarette, lit up and inhaled, holding his breath for a second before exhaling. I watched him watch the smoke's lazy upward drift. It was deliberate, slow, his deal for time. He was searching for words, at least the right ones, that he hoped to find before the trail of smoke—his prop—disappeared.

"Buddy," he finally said as he crushed the cigarette on the floor. "I gotta say somethin'."

"I know." I looked at the old man. He was solemn, and although I didn't know what he'd say, fears ripped me. Was he sick? Dying? He wasn't young anymore. The thoughts made me shiver. I braced for the worst.

"You know, Buddy, we got lotsa good times here," he said with a chuckle.

I nodded, glad that he hadn't found the right words. The message, whatever it was, was delayed. The old man·was relaxed now, maybe drifting into a land of dear and distant recollection where he was the young giver of gifts— gifts of priceless affection and patience, of candy and coin, and once, even a live chicken, a present from one of Uncle Leo's many farmworker friends.

"Remember the chicken?" I asked.

Leo smiled. "Of course," he said. "How can I forget?"

A young chicken in a box had briefly graced this room. Leo was to fatten the visitor, but he didn't have the heart. So the chicken became mine on the promise it wouldn't be stewed, fried, or soaked in vinegar. In our yard, in the middle of the city, it lived quietly until it (now clearly a male) flaunted its emerging sense of gender with a sunrise solo. My folks, unamused, threatened to eat the offender before mid-morning. I objected: "He's a pet!" Dad compromised. He knew a farmer who'd gladly provide a home. When the farmer arrived, I repeated my promise, hoping that he, too, would feel honor bound.

"You bet," he said with a smile as he carried the rooster away.

"Buddy," Leo said, interrupting my reverie. He was solemn again; he'd found the words. "Buddy," he said slowly, "I got married in Talisay."

I was relieved. He wasn't dying after all. It wasn't so bad. Marriage was what my parents wanted for him all along. I just wished he hadn't waited so long. Most likely his new love was a poor young girl from the country, less than half his age; other old-timers had come back with child brides. Love? Maybe not. But, in most cases, affection and care for the old man, and, for his new wife, a chance to come to America. Leo could do worse.

I smirked. "Okay, Uncle Leo, how old? Seventeen? If she's older, I'm disappointed. She's younger, right? Younger?"

"Twenty-nine," he said evenly.

I was surprised; she was older than most. Still, I laughed and threw him some trash. "Too ol'," I roared in my best and heaviest Filipino accent. "Trade 'er in. Young boy like you? Too much loving for ol' girl like dat. She got warranty? Girl dat old need warranty, like Sears. Mebbe break down. Den what?"

No response. No smile. Maybe I offended him? "Come on, Uncle Leo," I said softly. "Only kidding. Come on. When you bringing her here?"

"I'm not," he said.

I didn't understand. Maybe he was joking? But then I glanced at the old man. No smile. "But Uncle Leo," I said, trying to sound light. "We gotta take a look at her; check her teeth. She got 'em, don't she? Being an import an' all. You know, quality control. You know . . ."

He waved his hand, its movement ending my stream of garbage words to fill the void created simply by my uncertainty. He stared at me, locking his eyes onto mine. Lock secured, he started to speak.

"She's a good girl, Buddy," he said slowly, deliberately. "But she's the oldest and takes care of the family, a big one. They're close an' won' let 'er leave. And she's good, obedient, you know. So I says I'll stay. And why not? Don' got much, jus' a little, but it goes a long way there. Enough for a house, a small place down by the beach." He paused for a moment, making sure I understood, then continued. "But first, I tol' 'em, I gotta go back and tell my boy. Not right no other way."

He sighed. "Tha's why I'm here," he said. "Why I need to see you."

I stared at this man who'd meant so much to me for so many years. And I saw him as he once was, dapper and younger and full of himself (as they all were), with a smooth, unlined face, his hair thick and black. And then, at midpoint, traces of time— lines and flecks of gray—starting to show. And finally, I saw him now. Time had won, leaving behind an old man in a Chinatown room—like all the other old men. I knew what he wanted. Make it easy, I thought. The least I could do. He needed to go. "Uncle Leo," I began, trying to choose my words carefully. "Do you love her?"

He shrugged. "Wha's it matter?"

Damn. Leo wasn't making my task easier. I paused to search for the right words, the right question. "Uncle Leo," I finally said. "Is she good for you?"

The question must have surprised him. He didn't immediately reply; instead, his eyes swept the room. His gaze finally focused on the screen of the new color tv. "Yeah," he whispered, without looking up. "Yeah. Good enough."

"Then go," I said quietly.

He nodded his head. "This ain' easy, Buddy," he said, his voice starting to shake. "But your folks's right. This land's too hard for ol' men." He paused. "Ol' fools," he whispered, "like me."

Leo brushed his eyes with his hand and stared briefly at the floor before looking up. "Better go now, Buddy," he said, as he slowly rose to his feet. "Gotta pack, plane's leavin' tonight. Tol' the manager, keep wha' you want. Joke's on him, though. Forty years this land, got nothin', jus' junk. Two bags are mine; tv's yours. Tha's it."

That's it? More than twenty years together and that's it? I protested, or at least tried to. "But, Uncle Leo . . ."

"Tha's it, Buddy," he said.

"But . . ."

He shook his head. "Don' make it hard, son." He then unplugged the tv and handed it to me. "Here," he said. "My house don' got electricity."

I cradled the small set under my arm, much as I'd done in old times with scores of earlier gifts. Uncle Leo gently tugged on my arm. "Better go," he said. I nodded. We walked slowly toward the door. There, the old man turned toward me. He hugged me stiffly, for him an uncommon gesture. "Jus' one thing," he said, as he stepped back. "Your folks, good people," he said. "But I know 'em. They'll talk. 'Ol' Leo,' they'll say. 'Ol' fool.'"

"Don't worry, Uncle," I assured him. "Nothing from me. Who

knows? Maybe you're in California? Far as I know, maybe the moon?"

He smiled. "Tha's good, Buddy," he said. "Our secret? Jus' like ol' times?"

I nodded, and the old man beamed. We stood in the doorway, silent and sad, unsure what to do next. I broke the impasse and reached to close the door. "Better let you go," I said quietly and bussed him on his cheek.

I then turned to walk quickly down the narrow, poorly lit hall. At the top of the stairs I paused, my mind retracing my steps, straining to hear the echo of footfalls leading from and to an old room full of good times.

Lotsa good times.

A Manong's Heart

Back before Volvos and lattes, when Seattle was a fight town, my Uncle Kikoy was the sport's best fan. His one-room Chinatown apartment was a shrine to the ring, its walls plastered with the posed photos of boxers, from the famous ones—Louis, Robinson, and Pep (these he'd arranged in a triangle with Louis at the apex, like some blessed ring trinity)—to contenders, pretenders, and never-were prelim pugs.

He said he loved boxing because it was like life, or at least the life he knew. "Sometimes, Buddy," he told me. "You just gotta be hard."

When I was a kid, Uncle Kikoy was often my designated sitter, and on those lucky times, I'd listen spellbound to his eyewitness accounts of the legends he admired, the great bouts he'd seen. One Friday evening, he and I were sitting in front of his small black and white, watching a young hotshot contender—a Mexican kid from LA—dazzle his plodding, overmatched foe. The announcers were gushing; they'd all but crowned this kid the next champ, a great one surely, maybe one for the ages.

"Fast," I said.

Uncle Kikoy yawned like he'd memorized the hype. "Okay, I guess," he said with a wave of his hand. He then slumped in his chair, briefly closed his eyes, and smiled. "But not like Dado," he said softly.

"Dado?"

"Yeah," he said. "Speedy Dado." His look said memory and import; this odd name I should never forget. "Speedy, yeah Speedy." He whispered the name like a prayer. "The bes'. Ever." Strong words from a man who knew fighters. "I show you something," he said. Uncle Kikoy then rose and walked slowly to the closet. "Buddy," he said. "Twelve now?"

"Huh?" My attention was focused on the set, where a wild, overhand tenth-round right had reversed the hotshot's fortunes. The Mexican kid had slumped to the canvas. As the referee started to count, the kid's neck twitched. At four, he rested on his haunches; at six, on one knee. Where would he be at nine? ten?

Drawn by the screams of the announcers, I drew closer to the set. "I don't believe this!" one voice said. "He looks like, he looks like . . ."

"Twelve, Buddy?" my uncle asked.

I glanced at him. "Huh?"

"How old?"

"Ten!" a duet replied. Surprised, I turned back toward the screen. This fight was over. The Mexican was sitting in mid-ring, head down, towel draped over his head.

"See, Buddy," Uncle Kikoy said. "Not like Dado, not at all." He was standing by the foot of his bed, holding in both hands a brown scrapbook the size of a small desktop. Gently, he put it down—cradling it like a newborn, its contents fragile, so precious. He slowly turned each coarse page, savoring it before turning to the next. On some pages, he'd linger a bit longer; I followed his eyes going top to bottom once, twice, then again. He'd stop, sometimes chuckle, then move to another page, another key to memory.

When he'd run out of pages, he sighed and looked up. "Come here," he said.

I moved beside my uncle to see a small, wrinkled black-and-white photo of two young Filipinos wearing handwraps. One was in a boxing stance, hands high, eyes narrow—a picture of championship malevolence. The other stood apart, relaxed, arms at his sides; he had the face of a man stifling a yawn.

"That's me," he said, pointing at the menacing image. "The other one's your dad."

"Huh?"

"He didn't tell you?"

"Uh-uh."

"Your Daddy had talent," he said. "Quick, nice punch, both hands. Just no desire. Mostly, he like to dress up—you know, uh, dance, socialize. He like Indian girls. Me? Not so good with the girlies. They like your daddy better." He chuckled. "But I like to fight."

"Why?"

"Had to," he said. "Harder time then."

"What?"

"Just harder, Buddy."

For the next two hours, Uncle Kikoy guided me through a thrilling and violent new world, from his own menacing pose— taken, he said in 1929—to glowing newspaper accounts of Pancho Villa, Ceferino Garcia, Small Montana, Sammy Santos, Young Tommy, and, of course, the sainted Speedy. I counted a hundred fighters, maybe more, and Uncle Kikoy knew them all— their best fight, their best punch, when it was thrown, against whom. My journey was punctuated by his occasional demonstration of Dado's graceful footwork (side to side, in and out, "like Astaire") or the arc of a blow as it traveled its course; that's how Garcia took this guy or that.

As we neared the end of the scrapbook, a picture of a dazed, beaten fighter, a Pinoy, caught my eye. He was seated on the canvas, his vacant eyes staring at the lens.

"Uncle Kikoy," I said excitedly. "I know him, I know . . ."

"Yeah," he said. "Dempsey."

"Dad's friend."

"Mine, too," he said.

"He's the one who wants to buy me an airplane."

"Too much heart," he said.

"A Boeing 707."

"But no skill," he sighed. "Not enough, anyway."

No one knew or remembered Dempsey's real name; he'd carried "Dempsey" for so long. I'd often see him in Chinatown. One moment, he might be standing very still, chatting with a friend; the next, he might crouch, or feint, or roll his head. His friends, other old Filipinos, would just shrug. "Bells," one explained. "Still hearin' 'em."

Uncle Kikoy, who'd seen him fight, was more specific. "Too many punches," he said. "Jus' too many."

As I grew older, I started to spend more time away from Chinatown, away from Uncle Kikoy and guys like Dempsey. The last time I saw the old fighter was a few years back. He was heading uptown in a slow, arthritic gait—most likely to the corner of Third and Union. It was a sunny fall day, and there were other old Pinoys up there.

He passed me and I called his name, but he didn't hear. He continued walking, oblivious to all, mumbling as he made his way. That fall day he was in his own world, dressed up—the old guys all dress up—with no place to go. He was wearing a suit that looked older than me, and the streets were the same ones he'd walked decades earlier; it was a treadmill he'd never left.

Many of his friends had. Some had married and moved to the neighborhoods, away from downtown and Chinatown. Others had died. Still others had gone home—to the Philippines. He'd leave, too. Maybe he already has; I haven't seen him since. One of his friends said he'd died; another said he was in a rest home. Either way, he was off the treadmill.

The old man's full ring name, Young Dempsey, was supposed to invoke the image of the fierce heavyweight champion, Jack Dempsey. The heavyweight, as ring fans know, was successful; his namesake was not.

At least that's what Uncle Kikoy and the other old Pinoys said. And they should know. They'd seen or read or heard about them all, from Young Dempsey to Ceferino Garcia. All Filipino contemporaries, all fighters, all part of the past.

When my uncle and his buddies talked about fighters, I listened. I learned that Pancho Villa, a flyweight, was the first world champ. Great fighter, they'd say, but the greatest? Maybe Dado (Kikoy's favorite) or Ceferino Garcia, a middleweight champion. A middleweight champion? They'd nod; big for a Pinoy. I learned that Garcia was an overblown welterweight, had little style, and tended to fade in the later rounds. But he hit hard and had that whipping, wicked bolo punch even before Kid Gavilan, and the second Sugar Ray. And on occasion, the darn thing would land.

The old men had seen Speedy or Garcia in Stockton, or maybe Salinas or Pismo Beach. Memory fades. But it really didn't matter because, after a while, one country town looked pretty much like any other. And asparagus was the same, whether it was cut in Watsonville or Walla Walla.

In those days, Pinoys followed the crops. For most, it was the only work available. The life was hard, always on the move but without the Gypsy romance. In some towns, they were tolerated; in others, hounded and beaten. No matter, the job was the same: long lines of Filipinos working in the fields, often from darkness to darkness. In place by sunrise, they finished at night.

And not a woman in sight, at least not until the weekend. Weekends there were Saturday night dates with whores working taxi dances. In rented halls, Pinoys would line up again, but this time to dance with the ladies. Dad told me it was ten cents a ticket for a couple of minutes, a slow fox trot with eyes closed. It was a rare chance to feel something human and warm. My father figured it was a good return on a dime.

Monday in the field would come soon enough, and the Mondays after that. All tomorrow promised was an old age full of Mondays, bent and sweating on a white man's farm.

For many, escape from rural drudgery became an obsession. Some left for the cities with little more than bus fare and vague hope. But for those escapees, the cities had their own restrictive rules. In the 1930s, urban life meant busboy jobs and too many rooms that wouldn't rent to Filipinos. At least in the camps there was shelter, but there was no such guarantee in the cities. Leaving the fields meant entry to another hard arena. At best, it was a lateral move along the underbelly.

The borders of urban life were marked by cheap hotels, bunched closely together and isolated from the rest of the city. Along these borderlines, Filipinos were tolerated, their truncated world mapped by the street names in different towns, names that, of themselves, gave no hint of isolation or despair. If a Pinoy traveled from one city to another, his journey was as much from Temple to King Street as it was from Los Angeles to Seattle.

The poverty of the 1930s touched most people, and Filipinos were not exempt. From Dad and Kikoy and my other uncles, I learned their Depression stories, where doughnuts and coffee or fish-head soup were the best, sometimes only, meal of the day. Or where they'd stand outside a restaurant and peer through the window at men more fortunate.

And when the story was done, I'd wait for the laughter or the smile—the silver lining—because that's what had followed when they'd told other stories to me as a child. But Depression stories were different; there was no laughter, no smile. Not even the trace of one. If I'd been wiser, I'd have recognized the bitter, wordless message, the deep sense of betrayal hidden in the lines of the eyes and the tautness of the lips.

As young boys, someone lied to them, but it wasn't evident at the time. Or maybe they believed in dreams. They lived for this fable, this America of the mind, and they chased it across an ocean to its source. Little more than children, many still in their teens, they were blinded by the gossamer dreams of the young.

When the dreaming stopped, it was more than just the poverty of the Depression that embittered them. Surely that was bad, a time marked by scarce work and poor pay, but Filipinos were no strangers to hardship. Only the Pacific Ocean and a handful of years separated them from the deprivation of their peasant youth.

Most young Filipinos today are ahistorical denizens of the present; they carry few if any visions of the American past. Sources of knowledge—history books or fuzzy newsreels—are rarely consulted. The past is known chiefly by its symbols—the breadlines, the shanties, FDR. When it's recalled, it's clean and detached; for the most part, it's not recalled at all.

The old Pinoys, however, are different. They remember the

poverty, having survived it, and the grime, having worn it. And worse, they still relive the humiliation of being a Filipino in America. For them, America's promise—made in village schools—was broken. America the untrue.

And so, faced with the heat of the fields and the filth and overcrowding of city hotel rooms, many young Filipinos in the 1930s turned to boxing as a way out, a way up; they were lured by the money, but only partly. The prize ring also provided that rare chance to be judged as an equal, which every Pinoy craved. The ring suspended society's norms, those rules that embodied a racial and social order favoring color over ability, class over potential. In the ring, a Filipino could beat a white man with his fists and not be arrested.

Professional boxing's an odd sport, an anachronism, a throwback to the days of dogs, pits, and bears. Yet it persists because, at its core, it's brutal and honest, a contest of courage and skill. The rules are minimal and remarkably unchanged. The same is true of the equipment. Fighters have no face masks, shoulder pads, or kidney protectors; just gloves, mouthpiece, cup, trunks, shoes—and heart. In this game, money can't save; it never could.

Organized sport in America magnifies the insignificant, attaching import to games and contests. Undoubtedly it's silly, but the magnification endures and because of it, every contest is a potential morality play involving competion between religions, classes, or races.

A contest creates ample opportunity for symbols, and in a world of symbols, it's difficult for any group to claim supremacy when its champion has been beaten. In this competition, symbols are held dearest by those who hold the least of anything else. In the 1930s, the great Joe Louis proved this time and again. For Black America, Louis was more than a boxer, and his bouts were more than sporting events. When he destroyed Nazi Germany's Max Schmeling, Harlem danced. With his hands, he suspended reality. At best, it was temporary, but for those with nothing, it had to suffice.

It was once the same for Italians and Jews. It's still the same for hungry young black men, Mexicans, and Puerto Ricans. And it was the same for Filipinos. What Louis meant to African Americans, Garcia, Dado, Santos, and Young Tommy meant to Pinoys. Every victory shouted equality from a forum of respect and public acclaim.

From the champions to the obscure pugs perpetually scrapping for peanuts on undercards, the old men knew them. They knew their moves, shared their hopes, and basked in their bravado—from the glories of Garcia and Montana to the graceless, futile courage of fighters like Young Dempsey.

Cefarino Garcia died some years back in the warmth of southern California. He was old and revered, his place in history secure, and his family mourned his death. Even the boxing magazines paid tribute. By Pinoy standards, he died well. At least it wasn't from a seizure in a dark, cheap hotel room, with the body discovered three days later.

Our boxers of the past have all but disappeared, as have most of their fans—our fathers, uncles, and friends. But among the remaining few who saw them, certain imprints remain. Memories, vivid and strong, exist like old and favored photos propped in the corner of an old man's mind, a bit frayed along the edges, but honest and very dear. Slices of time, they are remnants of an era, as is the man who holds them close.

Is it any wonder, then, that one of the quickest ways to a Manong's heart is to talk fights and fighters?

My uncle Kikoy's passion for boxing was lifelong. One list-
less summer day, just a few months before he died, I was with
him in his room. As avid as a kid, he began to describe a new
favorite champion. He rose on unsteady legs to show me what
he'd seen: slip, double jab, uppercut, cross.

"Strong," he said excitedly. "Fast, clever."

I smiled. And so are you, Kikoy, I thought. As were his
compadres, as were they all.

Stephie

On a late Friday afternoon in May, I sat at my desk in my unlit classroom, buried in math projects I didn't want to review. With school almost over and grades almost due, I'd eventually go over them. Probably tomorrow. I always did, which didn't mean now, as I picked one up and just as quickly put it down, wrote checks on bills past due, and reread the AM sports section.

My lethargy, I guessed, was owing to the weather, hot and muggy like an August day in Memphis. Or maybe the years. After seven of them spent in public school classrooms, I was still young enough, but I was burned out, baked to an emotional crisp. The years had brought security and perks, protection against layoffs, a better paycheck. But with each year, the hook had sunk deeper, buried by the weight of more protection, more money, more equity on the mortgage.

For the last few years, near the end of school, I'd wrestled with the question: stay or leave? My much younger second wife, ever cautious and reasonable, had always talked me into staying, relying on arguments based on my shrinking idealism, my psychological need to be productive, our shared need to be realistic and to start thinking about having kids. All valid, but beneath her rhetoric I sensed her unstated premise, the core of the matter: two paychecks covered the note; one could cover the petition for divorce.

"Stay, Buddy," she said.

So I stayed, because summer brought respite, a chance to rationalize and renew, to lie to myself and get ready to start a new year, which would already have aged badly enough by October, that by Thanksgiving I was faking it again, hanging on, starting the slow countdown to summer.

Stay, Buddy. But maybe this time I wouldn't—marriage, perks, yet-to-be-born kids, and equity-building notwithstanding.

I stared at my desk. The pile of papers hadn't budged. Without my assistance, there would be no right to left movement of page after page of garbled equations—reviewed and graded—from one pile onto another. I stood up slowly and grabbed the papers. Tomorrow, they could move as well at home.

The sound of shuffled paper was broken by a knock at my door. The janitor, I figured. Nat was a nice man, a fisherman full of stories of big, wild red-striped trout landed in secret spots. I'd promised to join him. Maybe this year I would.

I sat back down and propped my feet on the desk. We'd kill time; he'd lie and I'd listen for an hour, maybe more. It was better than going home. "It's open, Nat," I said, without looking up.

The door opened. "I'm not Nat," said a woman's voice. "Hope I'll do."

I turned quickly to see her standing in the doorway, a silhouette in the fading light. She was tall and slender, five-seven, maybe more, wearing a loose white sundress and sandals.

"Invite me in, Buddy?"

I knew the voice, but knowledge brought only silence, at least for a moment. I was too stunned to reply.

"Stephanie," I blurted.

"Come on, Buddy," she said softly. "Aren't we just a bit

beyond formality?" She paused. "Well?"

I managed to nod. "Stephie," I finally said. She was my teen-age love, the first and maybe the best. When she left, I had a rip in my heart that managed to heal, but not all the way. As she approached, my pulse quickened to loosen the stitches that tightened, then slowly broke, one by one by one.

I lifted myself out of the chair. I gulped. "How . . . how'd you find . . ."

"My mom," she said cheerfully. "She heard from a Filipino friend of a Filipino friend who knew your folks and blah, blah, blah. You know the rest."

"Yeah."

"Buddy, after all this time, that all you can say?" she said as she hugged me.

What could I say? It was so long ago. I was naive and seven-teen; she was two years older, a beautiful woman of the world, selling men's apparel at the downtown Nordstrom's. There, she met the man she married, a guy from Chicago, and she left for his hometown. Before then, we'd dated. For her it was casual. It must have been; she'd cut me off so well.

And here she was again. I was stiff at first, awkward, unsure what to do. Slowly, I started to relax, to enjoy just feeling her body, sweet and firm and still familiar, pressing against mine. Like instinct, my reaction to her was automatic.

"Long time, Stephie," I murmured.

Even after so many years, images buried deep in a far corner of memory started to churn, then rise. Not all were pleasant.

"Why?" I asked abruptly, pushing myself away. I pulled the chair toward me and sat down.

As spoken, it was a single question; in truth, it was divisible. Why'd you leave me? Why'd you think we could just pick up again? Why'd you come back?

Ladies choice. Stephie, still standing, picked number three.

"I'm visiting my mom," she explained, unruffled by my brusqueness. "She's old and not well. Been trying to tell her to come back with me to Chicago. Got a big townhouse. Just me and her . . ."

"Your husband?" I asked.

She laughed. "Lost him years ago."

I was stunned. The marriage had seemed so perfect for a girl with a prostitute mother and a John Doe Filipino father. (The suspect list of possible fathers was long. "Could've been anyone," she once said, pertly. "Maybe even your dad.")

Stephie's husband, my successor in her affections, was a law student at Northwestern on a summer internship at one of Seattle's big downtown firms. He was a white guy whose folks had money. One afternoon she sold him an expensive silk tie. He soon returned to purchase three more and pick up a wife. I was in high school; I was broke; I had no chance.

"Dead?" I asked.

"Bored." She shrugged. "He was a tax attorney, a good one, at a big Chicago firm. Good money, great money in fact." She paused. "But you know, he started to get fat. The more he made, the fatter he got. Then he started going bald. But we were rich 'cause he was riding this rocket to nowhere and taking me along." Stephie paused and turned toward me. She was pouting, a pose reminiscent of Mildred, her mother. "But you know the clincher?" I shrugged. No idea. "He hated accordion music," she said, straight faced. "Couldn't stand it." Accordion music. I stifled a laugh. I'd hated it, too, but I'd never let on when Stephie and I were together. "Any kids?" I managed to ask.

She shook her head no. "After two years of this crap, I shut him out. Cold. First, I stuck him in the spare room, then I started sleeping in flannels. Thick, ugly ones. You know, the kid kind with booties. Had a drawer just full of 'em." She laughed. "Try gettin' some through that."

"Hard," I said, not amused.

"He finally got the idea," she said. "But one thing about marrying an attorney, you start picking up things. Important stuff. So when it came time, I got me the best asshole divorce lawyer his money could buy. By the time it was over, I almost felt sorry for my ex, but not enough to give him back his townhouse and that nice chunk of settlement cash."

Hard. But that was Stephie, who'd learned from Mildred just how to survive.

I'd known Stephie since childhood. Back then, I mostly ignored her. Mildred had the annoying habit of telling anyone who'd listen how special her daughter was. Her precious Stephie was so smart and pretty, so polite (at least to those who counted), and so impeccably dressed, always. Plus, she was half-white and played the accordion. She was too good for me and the rest of my raggedy Filipino friends. At about eight, courtesy of my buddies, I learned a new and appropriate phrase that I quickly used: Fuck you, Stephie.

Those three words had their effect. She vanished, even when she was there. At the Filipino social functions Mildred and my folks would sometimes attend, I might, from my permanent post at the food table, catch a glimpse of snoot and attitude gliding by. But that was all. By the time I reached ten, Stephie was gone, permanently, I assumed, lost to Magnolia, her new neighborhood. There, the neighbors were white, and for Mildred, who lived through her daughter, that meant better.

Our getting together again years ago was by accident. I was

downtown one early Saturday evening; Stephie was just leaving work. She recognized me first. "Fuck you," she said, by way of an introduction that led to two coffees and a Coke—and the last bus to her place. But that was then.

"What about you, Buddy?" she asked me. "You OK?"

"OK," I said, lying about my present, a job I hated, and my past, an ache, rationalized once but now recalled. To these pieces of my life, this stranger had no right.

"Heard you got married again. Just wanted to check for myself," she said, pointing to my wedding band. "Guess the rumor's true."

I shrugged.

"Nice woman?"

"Yeah," I said tersely, hoping that the edge in my voice would end this line of inquiry. It didn't.

"Does she make you happy?"

This time I just stared at her, ignored her question, and posed one of my own.

"Stephie," I finally said. "Why'd you come here?"

"My mom."

More exasperation. I took a deep breath. "Let me start again," I said. "Why did you come here, to this place, to see me?" I spoke slowly, carefully. We stared at each other briefly. My eyes, I'm sure, shot bullets. She blinked first.

"I missed you," she said softly.

I didn't reply. Instead, I fought the urge to gloat. I tried not to hear my mother's voice, screaming maxims deep in my gut that I'd absorbed over the years and made mine: about sleeping in the bed you make, about actions having consequences, about I told you so's running from the point of infraction until the end of time.

"Come again," I said evenly, as I continued to stare. I made sure my sigh was audible.

She cleared her throat. "I said I missed you," she said, this time a bit louder.

"Why?" I was careful to maintain the ruse with short replies and a flat tone purposely drained of traces of blood and caring.

This time she sighed. Head down, she walked slowly to my desk and sat on the edge. We faced each other, maybe two feet apart.

"Buddy," she said, "that first year back in Chicago, I knew even then I'd made a mistake. I didn't fit. I hated his family, all pomp and bullshit. I was his prize, Buddy, his goddam, exotic island girl. I had to lie about my past, about Mom dating a cannery, a migrant camp. I had to fit, Buddy, to be suitable for suitable occasions. Through it all, I started missing you; not all the time, just enough to make it worse. You've got no pretensions, Buddy. You're nice, considerate, funny. The more I remembered, the better you looked. I wanted to call or write, but I was scared. It took me this long to come here." I just stood listening, blank faced, mute, a shake of the head from side to side. Inside, a tempest was building; I was losing control.

"Don't be singin' that song," I said, surprised at the cold tone and the jagged rock-shaped words that flew out. I didn't want to go that way, at least not that hard. But once committed, I had to follow through, all head and heart shots, no flesh wounds. I inched my chair back; I needed room to fire.

"You set it up," I said. "And now you bitchin'? I don't get it. That was the goal, right? Marry a rich white guy and improve the race? Be his pampered, mostly white prize? Island girl? Damn, that's what you wanted, babe."

I stopped to catch my breath. Stephie was stunned; me too,

but I wasn't finished. "Take this weak shit back to Chicago and tell it to someone who cares. Maybe your ex got a cousin or brother. Tell it to him, or Hans, or Lars, or any Aryan on a bar stool. Just don't be bringin' it here to me."

Overkill, and I knew it. At the end of my outburst, decades in the making, I was hot and panting, like a killer on the scene. But Stephie wasn't dead yet. She had a salvo of her own.

"Fuck you, Buddy," she said angrily. "You're judging me, but who gave you the right? You and your poisonous little friends—you know, the ones who always used 'bitch' instead of my name—hey, you guys had it easy. Got a mom and dad to teach you. Even breeds like me, at least they had a father. Who was mine? You had uncles, Buddy. You had the Community. You had it made. It was easy for you to be who you are, to be Filipino. Mom and me were outcasts, Buddy. Lepers."

She stopped and stared at the far window. Her eyes were red. "Wanna trade, Buddy?" she said in a voice I could barely hear.

I felt ashamed and just shook my head. "No," I said.

The silence between us threatened to harden into a wall marking our last time together. I didn't want it to get that far. "Stephie," I began.

She didn't respond.

I tried again. "Stephie, I was wrong. But you gotta understand I was pissed you weren't here where you shoulda been. And over time, you know, you do little lies to get by. And I went on, least I thought I did till you walked through that door and sent me right back. It ain't easy seein' you," I whispered, " 'cause I missed you so damn much."

She made no move, at least not at first. Eventually, faint twitches at the corners of her mouth managed to form the weakest smile. She turned toward me. "Me too," she sighed. "I shouldn't have listened to Mom."

"What do you mean?" I asked, puzzled.

"Mom said to give you up and marry this guy," she said. "She liked you well enough, but she said you had no future. No Filipino did. She always said I should use my being half-white as an advantage. I could grab some rich guy and lie to him, tell him I was Spanish, Hawaiian, anything but what I was. Back then, I heard it all the time: Use your looks, flutter those eyes, don't end up like me . . ."

As she spoke, I studied her face, now fuller than what I recalled. At her eyes, large and brown, unfamiliar clusters of tiny straight lines touched the corners, each one marking the passing of time—wasted time, time apart. And below them, longer crescents. Seeing them saddened me. Unlike before, she was wearing makeup carefully placed to hide the years. When did she start?

Stephie had been prettier then, but even now, still pretty. This time I blinked.

"So I didn't," she continued. "I married him 'cause I was scared. I didn't want to end up like Mom." She was pensive for a moment before looking at me. "Buddy," she asked. "Can you understand?"

Up to now, she'd done her best to stay under control, to somehow check the overflow of emotions and memories as deep as my own. Message delivered, she started to sob, while I just sat there, my hands gripping the sides of the chair. I didn't know how to stop the tears.

"Stephie . . ."

I reached for her right hand and held it with both of mine before pressing it to my cheek. "Stephie," I said.

With her free hand she wiped her eyes. Her body shivered as

composure slowly returned. "You know," she said evenly, "I'm not even sure what I expected, what I wanted, by showing up here. Figured at least I could say I'm sorry and hope you don't hate me."

"I don't," I said, and meant it. "It's okay. All of that happened a long time ago."

"Good," she said and fell silent, her eyes fixed on the floor.

"All right," she finally said in a slow, deliberate cadence. "Maybe I was hoping for something more." She grabbed my left hand and turned it palm up. With her right forefinger, she touched my wedding band. "Guess I'm too late, huh?" she said and gazed at me.

Truth or dare. I chose to abstain.

Her smile this time was more than faint twitches. "Maybe not," she said and pulled gently on the ring, which smoothly slid off. I didn't resist. She examined the band, then threw it to a far corner of the room.

"Stephie," I protested weakly, as she drew me toward the desk, and to herself and a passionate embrace too long delayed. As we kissed, my right hand dropped to lift ever so slightly the hem of her dress. Instinct again.

"Here?" she asked.

"Here."

"You're a bad boy, Buddy," she whispered as she pulled me down among the hated stack of papers that crumpled and fell, but finally moved.

She giggled. "You know, we could be related."

"Then maybe we'll have to sort it out," I said. "Tomorrow."

A Matter of Faith

When the phone rang, I knew I should've let it be. Bad news travels at 2:00 A.M. Still I picked up the receiver, driven by habit, not caution or sense.

"Buddy."

"Hi, Mom," I said, trying to sound cheery. "What's up?"

"Buddy, " she said sadly. "It doesn't look good."

My heart dropped; I could barely make a sound. "What?" I finally said. It was the best I could do.

"Your uncle Kikoy. He went to intensive last night, you know, for his heart. He wants to see you, just in case."

I loved my mom, but I'd learned life from my dad and his cronies, those stylish, confident, generous men who'd taught and protected me, kept me safe. Wherever. Chinatown cardrooms, flophouses. Wherever. But for those happy, secure times, there was a price to pay. I would mourn more than the passing of my two parents. Uncle Kikoy, I knew, was just the first of many.

"They're all going, Buddy . . ." She started to cry. "Every week we attend funerals. Seems that's all we do. All the old-timers, our friends."

I sighed. "I'll be up, Mom," I said, as I reviewed a mental ledger drowning in red: some cash in, more cash out. What cash was left I was saving, or trying to save, for something big, something as yet undetermined—maybe a down payment on a house, maybe a new car. Maybe a new pair of tennis shoes. Saving was a reflex action learned when I was young. "For the future," my mother would say. Here in Frisco, almost thirty years later, the future had come and gone. But still, I saved.

Flying was out of the question, not on short notice. I couldn't afford it. Skeptical ticket agent: "Round trip to Seattle? Costs more than you'll ever have."

Alternative two: Greenie, my twenty-year-old beater. I wondered if it could last the distance from Frisco to Seattle. Greenie might not return. But for this journey, one way was enough. The trip would be tough, no doubt, but I had no choice. Uncle Kikoy was family, the bottom line.

"Buddy," she said. "When you coming?"

"Soon as I can," I told her. There'd been other motor trips north. I'd done it before, in fact several times, but never alone, and never during December. Silently, I computed costs: gas, oil, tuneup, food . . . scratch food, just drive straight through. "Two days," I assured her. "Three days max."

"Buddy," she sighed, "he might not last that long."

"Tell 'im to wait," I said. "Uncle Kikoy will wait. Just tell 'im it's a matter of faith; his boy's comin' home."

It's a matter of faith, I thought, as I ran through the automatic doors and into the lobby of the VA Hospital. My uncle Kikoy had been a sniper in the Pacific War—his job: to pick off remnants of the Japanese Army in the jungles of Borneo, Samar, and Leyte. He apparently enjoyed his work. "When I aim, they see their ancestors," he'd say proudly. He'd laugh, more a high-pitched giggle—and roll up his right sleeve to show a scar in mid-bicep. "Of course, they try to make me see mine. But, you see, I'm not dead 'cause I got faith." He'd point to his heart. "In here, Buddy. In here."

In that sense, Uncle Kikoy differed from most of the other old-timers, an irreligious lot. I never saw him in a church, but he believed in God and summoned Him periodically. "You got problems, Buddy," he'd say solemnly, "you ask for help. It'll come. The Japanese, they shoot at me, but they miss 'cause I believe. It's a matter of faith." On those occasions (and there were several), I'd nod, feigning agreement. Even as a child I wasn't religious; as a young man, even less so. I saw no need for God. He was illogical, worse, inconvenient, especially after I'd started dating—a diet of Catholic schools nothwithstanding.

Still, I survived those days, and around my neck I still wore a symbol from an earlier time: the small Saint Christopher medal Uncle Kikoy had given me when I turned eight. He was wearing it, he told me, the day he was shot. It had saved him when he was young; Saint Chris was good at that, based on his record with the traveling Baby Jesus. But now, he told me, he was old (over fifty years to my eight) and getting older; last he checked, not even saints could stop the movement of time. I, however, had a long way to go. And on that road, Saint Chris could be helpful.

Out of respect to Uncle Kikoy, I wore the medal, but in all those years I never invoked the power of my holy protector. A narrow, unbending logic was enough; all else was superstition. Still, during that time I also never once removed it from around my neck, and I'd managed to survive bouts of recklessness and prolonged adolescence. I'd even survived the sixties and its two-decade sequel, somehow managing to stumble through a deep purple haze, leaving friends, family, and wives in my wake. When I came to, I was single again, this time in Frisco in a one-room walkup, nursing a headache that outlasted an era. But I was lucky; I knew others who never got that far. Saint Chris must love fools, even old ones.

The medal dangled from my neck on the morning I raced from the parking lot into the hospital where my uncle lay, maybe minutes from death. I was late. It had taken three days just to gather the money, buy the parts for my car, do the repairs. Even then, nothing was assured.

"Nurse it," Herbie had said. A reformed car thief, he was, like many of his trade, a superb underground mechanic, maybe the best in Frisco. He was the older brother of Junior, my next-door neighbor. Herbie ran an unlicensed garage out of their parents' house, and he was so good his customers included lawyers, judges, even cops. I'd seen him somehow squeeze miles out of rusting engine blocks; two years before, Greenie's odometer had frozen at a quarter of a million miles. I needed more.

He frowned as I counted the bills. "Two hundred," I finally said, and thrust the cash toward him.

Herbie just shook his head and made no move to accept payment.

"Did the best I could, bro," he said. "But I can't guarantee."

"Got a chance?"

Herbie shrugged. "A chance," he said. "Donner Party had a chance."

"Wrong mountains," I said.

"Principle's the same, " he replied. Although he laughed, he'd made his point. Even with a new car, a midwinter trip through the mountains was never easy.

"A chance's all I need," I said, and again tried to hand him the money.

Herbie shook his head. "Nah. It's all uphill from Redding on," he said, referring to the long, winding route from northern

California to central Oregon. "You get stuck there, brother, you'll need all the coin you got. That happens, man, stay away from hungry-lookin' toothless hillbillies. They'll eat you, Buddy. It's cultural." He paused. "Pay me when you get back."

"Herbie, man . . ." I stuttered, trying to thank him.

"Forget it," he said. "From one Flip to another. Means I understand. Got uncles like Kikoy. Different names, same situation. Go on. If you're like me, you owe 'im."

The trip became a twenty-hour ordeal. Along the way I'd stop to call collect. Status checks. The last was from Grants Pass at midnight, ten hours into the trip. "He's OK," my mother had said. "Resting. But hurry."

I did the best I could, particularly with the oil leak that had sprung as I crossed into Washington. With one eye on the oil light, the other on the road, I ignored the grind of metal on metal and a headache that screeched almost as loud. Somehow I shut it all out and pressed on, never stopping, didn't dare to, especially in the homestretch—from Tacoma to Seattle—when Greenie sputtered forward on will and occasional bursts of downhill momentum.

One more time, Herbie's magic had worked. I'm not sure how he did it—maybe duct tape, superglue, and two novenas. Maybe Saint Chris. What mattered was that my faithful Greenie—now a collection of loosely joined parts—was in the hospital parking lot, and I was standing by the front desk in the lobby.

"Kikoy's room," I blurted to the receptionist, a bored-looking woman chewing vigorously on a large wad of gum. Cow with cud, I thought. She was staring at the last down space of a newpaper crossword of stunning simplicity. I glanced at the down: a five-letter synonym for "fake."

"Pardon me?"

"I'm sorry," I said, trying to gather myself. "I mean . . . Rodriguez, Mr. Rodriguez." I suddenly realized I'd never known Uncle Kikoy's real first name.

"Which one?" she asked blandly, without looking up. She was tapping her pencil and thumbing through a small pocket dictionary. "We have many patients with that last name, at least four as of yesterday."

Damn, I thought. I didn't know his first name. To me, he'd always been "Kikoy"—a nickname. For Filipinos, nicknames meant closeness, a key granting access to the intimate. I didn't know his real name, didn't have to. I blinked and looked nervously at the clock, trying not to look dumber than the woman in front of me.

"Never mind," I finally said. "What's the floor for intensive?"

"Third floor." She yawned and pointed to the elevator down the hall.

As I hurried toward the twin elevator doors, I looked backward over my shoulder. "Try 'phony,'" I yelled at the woman. She looked up, unsure. "You know," I added, "like the folks who work here."

The elevator opened to the third floor and a familiar voice. "Wait," the voice commanded before I could exit. A thick right hand firmly grabbed the edge of one door, keeping it open for my mother to enter. My father followed. Downcast, they didn't notice me, surely a bad sign.

"Mom," I whispered.

She looked up. "Buddy!" she cried as she hugged me. Dad was always reserved; he patted me on the shoulder. "He's gone," she said sadly. "You missed him. He asked and he asked, and I told him to hang on, that you're coming, but he couldn't . . ."

"Mom," I said, gently trying to loosen her grip, "I should at least see the body, do somethin' . . ."

"Can't," she said. "Body's gone; moved it an hour ago." She paused. "There's nothing more to do."

"Damn," I whispered. Nothing but hope and its helpers—caffeine and adrenalin—had kept me going this far, and I'd finally run out. Busted car, broken spirit. I leaned against the wall, legs shaking, too tired to stand, too sad to move. My system was shutting down. "Damn." It was all I could say.

"Just come on home, son," my mom said. She held my arm tight. "You need to rest. Don't worry about Uncle Kikoy. He knows you tried. I told him you were coming, and he'd smile. As the end got closer, I'd tell him, beg him to hang on. And he'd still smile, 'though I'm not sure he even heard the words."

My mom paused and pulled me closer. "Just before he died," she whispered, "he said something to me. He knows I'm religious, just like him. Your father's not." I glanced at Dad, who stood away from us, back straight, hands folded, head up, eyes focused on the elevator doors. At seventy plus, he was a proud, still physical man who fought the frailties of age—the crooked fingers, the curved backs of his friends. Mom claimed he willed his bones to stay straight, and I believed her. His hearing, though, was another matter. It was almost gone. He had a hearing aid, but pride kept it out of his ear and in a drawer.

"Go ahead, Mom," I said in a normal tone.

"Anyway, he doesn't know," she said, still whispering. She nodded at Dad. "Your father was out in the hall. Kikoy said, 'Tell Buddy, don't worry,' he says. 'I'll see 'im. I got faith. But he gotta have it, too.'"

I stared at her blankly.

She shrugged. "Exact words," she said.

As the elevator doors opened, Dad suddenly turned to me. "Jus' come home and rest," he said. "Think about tomorrow, tomorrow. Nothin' more to do here, Son."

"Nothin' more to do," I managed to mumble. "Least not here."

In the dark my heart raced. I could hear it, louder and faster, revving to a level I knew it couldn't keep. Then what? Wake up, I thought, and turn it down.

Eyes opened to adjust to a dim light from two small candles on the desk by the wall of my old bedroom. Quickly, I sat up and pledged allegiance to a hope that the rhythm of my heart was normal. Okay. I glanced at my watch. Almost midnight, twelve hours of sleep, a lot. That night, though , I wanted, needed more. But the puzzle lingered: why the odd, pounding, cardiac dream?

No answer, at least not at first, as I stared at the tiny flames that flanked a small picture of Jesus, His heart wounded and choked by a crown of thorns. No doubt, my mom's handiwork. She believed in prayer, of which lit candles and religious pictures were a form. Each room in the house had a similar shrine, although mine had been removed at the onset of puberty—when I found sex (or at least sexual thoughts) and lost faith—till the day I left home. Fire hazard, I'd successfully argued. Now, after my long absence, my mother was back to her tricks, praying for me even while she slept.

I smiled at the thought, God or no, and smiled also at the other lessons that this kind, believing woman had tried vainly to impart. I couldn't remember them all, there were so many, now tangled like a collection of old fishing lines. I'd sort them out in the morning, too tired now to ponder religion, the meaning of the dream, or any other matter.

As I started to slide back under the covers, one candle went out. I blinked. Odd. No flicker, no sign the flame would soon extinguish. Then the second. Same way. Eerie, much worse than odd. I bolted back up, my mind racing to find an answer, a logical one. Fatigue, imagination, bad eyesight? Maybe a breeze? A quick scan of the walls searched for open windows; slight cracks would do. Then I remembered. My religious mother was also energy conscious—this house was hermetically sealed, a double-paned PG&E temple.

I slumped in the bed, out of answers, except answers I didn't want. Eyes open, too scared to sleep, I could only breathe and stare. A small lamp on the bedstand tempted me; electricity—that natural marvel—could break this dark, superstitious grip. Light could bring rational answers, buy time enough to analyze and reduce, maybe even to forget. I reached for the switch, then stopped. What if light explained nothing?

I withdrew my hand.

My mind returned to the same circle of futile inquiry—fatigue, imagination, bad eyesight, a trick of shifting air. Ponder, discard. Once. Ponder, discard. Again. There was a fifth explanation. This I fought, preferring safer, more logical choices. But fear exhausts, destroying resolve, inviting the unwelcome message from the past morning: Uncle Kikoy would visit if I had faith.

I loved Uncle Kikoy and I wanted to see him, but at what cost? Should I invoke Saint Chris to bring him, my uncle, now a phantom, no longer flesh and bone? Then what? Attend church? Relearn rules and rituals long dismissed as inconvenient bunk?

Grabbing the medal, I ripped it from my neck. I held it up to a dim thread from a streetlight filtered weakly through double glass panes. I closed my eyes and felt the contours of Saint Chris, maybe my guide through a logical fog of ponder and discard.

The medal was a gift from family, an act of kindness, one of many not yet repaid. And here was a chance. Uncle Kikoy was family, the bottom line. I owed him. For the first time that night, I relaxed. Then I laughed. All this fuss, and there was really no choice. Carefully, I laid the medal on the bedstand and got ready to pay a debt.

I closed my eyes and could feel my palms dampen. I hesitated, gripped by no small fear. Again, my heart started to pound, revving like a modified Detroit V-8 on Saturday night. Breathing deeply, I gathered myself and plunged ahead.

For family, the bottom line.

"Just bring 'im, Saint Chris," I said, hearing my words over my own internal din. Then silence, broken by a faint sound, probably imagined—a trace of a giggle, high pitched.

I gulped. "Bring 'im," I whispered.

Dancer

In the Northwest, when the rains come, the creeks flood and steelhead swim the highways and rest on top of cars. Last year, the day before Christmas, was such a day. I was in downtown Seattle on First Avenue, dodging traffic, running hard against the light. I was hoping to reach a dry oasis—a pawn shop awning—across the street from the starting point of my ankle-deep dash. I made it and took stock of the damage. To my surprise, I was fairly dry, but I wouldn't be for long if I stepped back into the downpour. I shrugged, lit a smoke, and started to survey the watches, jewelry, knives, and guns arrayed in the window.

As a boy, I'd always loved pawn shops, most of them here on First, in the heart of Skid Row. They'd seemed so full of strange, forbidden things, and for a moment the old fascination returned, lured this time by a German luger, once owned (the ad claimed) by one of Hitler's senior advisers. Above it was a row of curved swords, serrated knives, and sleek black daggers, assassins' tools, often and recently employed, or so I imagined.

I chuckled and glanced at my watch; it was late—half an hour had passed—and, judging by the light patter on the awning, the rain had lessened. I figured I'd better leave now before the deluge returned. I took a last quick look at the pawn shop window—and caught the reflection of two faces, not one, abutting like a bad sepia snapshot of kids jammed into a photo booth. The second, a woman, was older but very pretty, and vaguely familiar despite the sunglasses, odd attire for a dark, drenched day.

"Buddy," the woman said. "Is that you?"

I blinked but didn't immediately respond. Instead, I carefully examined the image in the glass. "Sonia," I finally said. I turned to face her; it had been too long. After so many years, I was stiff and formal, unsure what to do next.

Sonia solved that as she brushed past my outstretched hand. "Little Brother," she scolded. "All this time and you're gonna shake my hand?" She grabbed me in a hug so strong, I gave ground and felt the pane against my back.

"Careful, girl," I said. "Any more affection and we'll be part of the display." She laughed and squeezed harder. "Right next to the watches," I added. "Knives and shit be stickin' us."

"Wouldn't want that." She laughed again and slowly started to loosen her grip. "I've wondered about you," she said softly as she stepped back.

"Me, too," I mumbled, studying her. She was tall, even without the blue stiletto heels. Bright red leotards, short black leather jacket, and wide brimmed hat completed her attire. A hooker's winter gear? I was too scared to ask.

"Nice sneakers." It was all I could say.

Sonia placed her hands on her hips. "Relax," she laughed. "I don't walk no streets, at least no more. She paused. "Ain't no ho, honey. I'm an artist."

My reflexive nod didn't fool her.

"A dancer, Buddy," she added impatiently. "And if you just keep standin' there noddin' with your mouth open, you gonna make me late." She grabbed my arm. "But we still got time, you can buy me a cup."

Our destination was a corner table at a fast food joint a few doors down. For a moment, it was just like old times—Sonia, my protector, leading me from one neighborhood point to another. And like old times, I relaxed and just followed. But one day she was abruptly gone from our family, and I mourned her loss. Despite my questions, my parents never explained.

Yet even before she'd gone, there were signs that all wasn't right. She'd leave for days, sometimes longer, always in the company of an adult, a tall, thin Filipino. Then, just before she finally disappeared, I saw her cry one day. I asked why. She hugged me close and said I'd be fine, just fine, cross her heart.

We used to have pictures: smiling little brother/big sister black-and-whites. Sonia at ten, fine dark features, high cheekbones, black curly hair; me, six years younger, Chinese eyes and moon-pie face, a physical yin and yang. Most of the photos disappeared in the days after she'd left. But one I'd managed to save; I'd carried it with me since, awaiting a time that was finally here.

"Remember this?" I asked, as Sonia sipped her coffee. I handed her the photo, now old, wrinkled, fragile as a communion host. Gently she took it betwen her thumb and forefinger and held it to the light. She studied it like a relic, a key to our past. "Remember where?"

"Woolworth's," she said quietly. "Picture booth, 'bout two blocks from here. 'Bout this time, too."

I smiled. As she handed back the photo, she started to shake. "I'm sorry," she whispered and grabbed a napkin to dab the corner of an eye. I waited; I still had a question to ask.

"Why'd you leave?"

"Buddy," she said evenly, "it wasn't my choice."

"What do you mean?"

Her eyes shot from side to side. "I'm late," she said. "We

don't have time . . ."

"Time enough."

"Later," she said, and rose quickly to leave. "I'm late."

"Please," I pleaded as she walked toward the door. "Almost forty years now, and I still don't know why you left." I paused. "You left me, you know. Me."

Sonia was almost out the door when she stopped. She turned and walked slowly back toward the table. "Gimme a cigarette," she said casually. "I know you smoke, bad boy. Seen the pack hangin' out your jacket." I handed her a Marlboro. She sat down, lit up, and quickly took a drag, leaning forward. Her pursed lips pushed a small gray cloud my way. I blinked. "Bullseye," she giggled. "I'ma tell Dad. Bad habit, you know."

I coughed and nodded.

Sonia leaned back in her chair and exhaled once more. "It's a long story, Buddy." She sounded weary, almost indifferent, as she watched the smoke lift lazily upward to touch the ceiling then disappear. A long, twisted, shadowy trail of blood ties and memory. I said nothing and just waited for her to return.

"You ready?" she finally asked. She laid her arms on the table and stared at me as she spoke. "Buddy, you might not like what I say," she cautioned. "But if it's go, let's go."

A chill raced up my spine, but I nodded nonetheless. "Let's go," I whispered.

For almost four hours she talked, and the story she told was sad and sometimes angry, but mostly resigned. In no particular order, she moved from one episode to another, her words forming a string to connect the uncharted points of an unfathomed, common past. Some things I knew ("Buddy, we got different moms. Mine's Indian and died just after you was born, so I came to live with Dad"); some I didn't ("You got three other half-brothers and sisters, Buddy, at least by my mom. Knowing Dad, I'm sure that ain't all.")

Recent years had seen her move from one hard set to another: abusive lovers, an unwanted pregnancy, life on the streets, her child grabbed by the state. After that, she figured her current job, as an exotic dancer, was an improvement. "Least I'm indoors," she said. "Bein' cold's the worst part."

She sighed. "It's been hard, but it's better now. Tips're fine'n all, and at least I ain't hookin'; plus, Baby Brother, I'm good, real good." she chuckled. "You know, old but bad. To the bone, Buddy, down to it. Black girls? Shit. Young bitches? Fuck 'em. Got nothin' on me."

As I listened, my heart left me to join her caravan of words traveling a bleak emotional desert, the toll of which was about to be paid. Sonia was now quiet, as tears started to fall down both sides of her face. She didn't try to stop them. Instead, she threw her head back and signaled with the index and middle fingers of her right hand.

"Thought you said it was bad," I said, and handed her a lit Marlboro.

She smiled. "It is."

I waited until she finished her smoke. I had a question, the same one—in four hours, she still hadn't answered it.

"Sonia," I asked. "Why'd you leave?"

She sighed and breathed deeply. Maybe she wouldn't respond? "Buddy." she finally said, "I don't blame your mom. I know you're close . . ."

"Sonia!" I said, interrupting her. My sharp tone said I wanted the answer, damn the cost.

"She didn't want me, Buddy," she said flatly. "Never did. Never said nothin' to me, but I knew." She paused and wiggled her fingers. I handed her another smoke. "She wanted me gone."

I stared at her, dumbfounded, not at all sure what to do next. I was close to my folks. Especially my mother. I gagged an urge to scream, to demand proof, to curse both the slander and the slanderer. I managed to catch myself, recalling that I'd summoned the words just spoken. Instead, I pulled out a cigarette, lit it, dragged on it slowly, and looked at her. She too, was unsure, wondering if she should continue, wondering if she'd gone too far.

I touched her hand. "Go on," I said softly.

"Buddy, I . . ."

"Go on."

Sonia nodded. "Remember Alex, that tall, skinny Filipino?"

"Yeah."

"He was my mom's last boyfriend before she died. Him and Mom had two other kids, and after she passed, I'd go stay with 'im for part of the summer. Mostly, Alex used me to babysit, while he'd get drunk . . ."

"What happened to the kids?"

"Don't know," she said softly. "Lost track, but hey, that's nothing new." She sighed and dabbed again at her eyes, trying hard not to lose it. She succeeded, at least at the start.

"Mom had a will done and left Alex some money," she said calmly. "It was for me, really, but he couldn't touch it unless I was livin' with him. So one day he asks Dad, and the next . . ."

She stopped and scanned the room, her eyes blinking hard and starting to water.

"'Scuse me," she said, and took a deep breath. "The next day I was gone."

"Sonia," I said. Watching her these few moments, I realized that the cost of my question might have been too high. Answering hurt her too much; her words, painful to her to think about, must have been unbearable to say. Too late, I regretted my inquiry.

"Sonia . . ."

"Gone," she said in a tiny voice, barely a whisper. "I can't blame your mom—I'm sure when Dad went back to the Philippines he didn't tell her about me or the others he helped put on this earth. Maybe she pressured 'im, I don't know. Plus, we were poor with more on the way. Remember? Your mom was pregnant."

"Yeah."

"Her, I can understand. It's Dad. All this time and I still can't figure how he could just turn his back, give me up like some damn donation. Without a fight, Buddy, not even an explanation."

She paused, her voice so mournful and true it touched, then crossed, then covered my heart. I rubbed my hand across my eyes. "Buddy, I'm his flesh and blood," she said, "just like you. And the bitch is, I still love 'im."

What could I possibly say? I had no answer to her answer; I recovered, but just barely. "Another cup?" I said weakly.

"Yes," she mumbled.

I rose for her refill and welcomed the break. When I returned, she thanked me for the coffee. We talked a bit more—chitting and chatting—but said very little. We'd already said too much. Sonia seemed relaxed; she laughed at my jokes and nonsensical puns. We traded phone numbers, promising to stay in touch. This time the words were pleasant and harmless, good only for killing time, the countdown to the end of our time together.

She moved first, a glance at her watch. "Damn, almost midnight," she said as she gulped the last drop of coffee. "Way late, but it goes twenty-four hours, so I'll get my time." She chuckled. "'Sides. I shake plenny butt like Tina Turner, my patron saint. Gotta work this money-maker. Little Brother, my public is waiting."

"Even on Christmas Eve?"

"Yeah," she laughed. "Even on Christmas Eve. Besides, watchin' me's better'n hangin' out here."

Without another word, we both rose and walked toward the door. Sonia took my hand and led me, just like before. Just like always.

Outside, the rain had stopped, replaced by a cool, fine mist that welcomed pause and conversation. I felt awkward, didn't know what to say. She reached over to kiss my cheek. "Sonia," I said, blurting it out. 'Why don't you come with me, see the folks, it's Christmas . . ."

She shook her head. "Can't, I . . . just too many years, too many damn Christmases." She paused. "Know what I mean?"

My sigh said I knew what she meant.

"Buddy," she said softly. "One more thing. You ain't seen me. This ain't happened? Okay?"

I shrugged, perplexed. "Sure, I guess . . ."

My qualified answer triggered a lecture. "Buddy, it ain't like I'm a damn doctor, or scientist, or somethin'. 'Sides, for all this time, they ain't never asked about me, and I ain't about to start fillin' 'em in." She paused to make sure I understood. "So I'ma tell you, this ain't happened. Okay?"

"Okay."

"Cross your heart, Buddy."

"Damn, Sonia," I muttered.

"Cross it, Little Brother," she said sternly.

Heart finally crossed, she smiled and kissed me again, then abruptly turned away. I watched her go, walking her dancer's walk—butt swaying to a silent rhythm—off toward a doorway two blocks down. Above the door, a huge neon sign proclaimed the presence of live girls and entertainment that never stopped, not even on Christmas. I watched her go.

I had to head for the bus stop, two corners down, the opposite way. The last coach was due to leave at 12:15, in five minutes. But there was something I had to say that I hadn't remembered to say, that it was too late for her to hear me say. I said it anyway, real softly.

"Merry Christmas, Sis."

A Family Gathering

As I walk along the edge of the neatly trimmed lawn, I hear, (and feel) the opening notes of the annual fall sonata. It's October in Seattle and the rains will come as they always have; I was born here and know the patterns well. And although I've been away, old responses quickly return. I pull down my cap, turn up my collar, and just keep walking as the first few drops touch my neck and face, then stop. I chuckle. It's a feint, an old trick. The gentle scout drops are a portent of the deluge to come. At the end of my walk, I'll be soaked to the bone.

But I don't mind, because it's pretty here—all flowers, grass, and trees. Ringing the far border, a tall surrounding hedge creates in me a sense of separation and solitude, an appropriate response for a cemetery stroll. But not sorrow, because I'm going to a gathering of men that I love.

My father's death surprised me. It shouldn't have; he was eighty-seven years old. But I thought he'd live forever, as would his brothers, cousins, and buddies—my uncles—who came to this land long decades ago, when racism and violence, migrant poverty, tuberculosis, and despair should have killed them, but didn't. Such forces, the afflictions of the poor, didn't even wrinkle the creases of the zoot suits they wore while standing on corners, from Seattle to LA, where they'd laugh and talk loud, welcoming the night.

But of course they die just like the rest of us, which, of course, they weren't. At least not like those of us lucky enough to have been born here, and not like the new generation of educated immigrants who came thirty years later from the Philippines and landed on a much softer place. The latter had trunkloads of degrees and well-founded hope, even titles (Dr. Alvarez, Attorney Fernandez, Engineer Rufina) far more impressive than the ones held by their predecessors (Asparagus-Cutter Vera Cruz, Fish-Sorter Daan, Short-Order Cook Cavinta).

The newcomers didn't know what the old men had done and, quite frankly, couldn't care less. They wouldn't see the connection between their own comfort and what others had struggled to build. They couldn't see that the old men had heart and did the most with the least, and with a style they can never have and that I'll never see again.

It's been sixty years since Dad and his peers arrived, and now they're going, one by one. At first the passings were distant—acquaintances, relatives of friends, other old-timers known only by rumor—but now, it's the last rush to the gate. At the start I couldn't see the end, but now I can, and I mourn their leaving.

Uncle Kikoy was the first. With my father, he'd come to this land toting nothing more than a sack full of hope, soon gone and buried by the dust of migrant jobs. That was his life and, depending on the season, he was planting or cutting asparagus, or canning salmon, a half-century cycle broken only by time spent shooting at Japanese soldiers in the Pacific. When he first came to Seattle, he stayed in Chinatown—a place for the poor and the colored—in a one-room hot-plate walkup. Between jobs, he'd always return to that room; I met him there forty years ago.

"Your uncle," my father said. "He'll watch you." A few years back when he passed, I swore in a prayer I'd never forget him. It's a promise I've kept. In the time since, whenever I've come home to Seattle I've stopped by his grave and said a prayer, if I had one, or laid a flower or a coin on his headstone, or just said "hi" and lit a smoke. As rituals go, it's hardly elaborate, nothing profound or eloquent. But then, Uncle Kikoy and I didn't talk much in life; his English was bad, my Cebuano was worse. Still, as a kid I just liked hanging around him; I felt safe there in his Chinatown orbit as we strolled by bars and cardrooms, and that feeling stayed with me through the years. Boy and man, I just liked hanging around him. His death hasn't changed it.

The promise I made to Uncle Kikoy, I made also to my father, who, just this year, was buried not twenty yards from his cousin. Unlike Kikoy, Dad's English was passable, which allowed him to jump me every time I screwed up a math assignment, and later, marriages and careers. "Your name," he'd hiss, and shake his head. "It's who you are, who we are. Don' never shame it."

Of course I ignored him as I gathered shame by the bucket. And of course he was right and I knew it, even as I marched through bogs of weakness and poor judgment, journeys of the young. Of course he was right; he'd earned his name the hard way as a teenage immigrant with nothing to start, but with a church full of mourners to finish. Their hymns of sorrow, impassioned and pure, formed a shroud around my father and lifted him away. I didn't see it, but I felt it. I swear it happened just that way.

Would the same songs be sung for me? I wonder. True enough, I carry his name, but only by accident of birth.

I am now on familiar ground, the northeast corner of the

cemetery. I recognize the names; other Filipinos are here as well. There's Manong Fabian, twenty years our neighbor, twice that our friend. It's like our old neighborhood, reassembled plot by plot; all that's missing are the sounds—the laughter and the mix of dialects and accents inviting me in, to dinner or just to visit. Friends in life, we've chosen to be together again.

Under the awning of a small brick mausoleum, I light up and sit, waiting for the rain, now windwhipped and horizontal, to pass. It's too strong, even for a Northwest native. I could be here ten minutes or two hours; it doesn't matter. Dad and Uncle Kikoy are nearby; I can feel them.

Dad's presence here has made it official. A quorum has convened for a gathering of my family whose full list of members has not yet arrived. Typical of such gatherings, some are stragglers, excused by comparative youth (Mom, at seventy) or sheer stubbornness (Uncle Vic, at ninety-one). But eventually, they'll be here, all of them who, decades ago, faced a hostile land and didn't even blink. It's another reason to come home to Seattle. But I can't, at least not yet. There's no work here. Maybe in a few years. For now, I'll just have to visit when I can, especially as the roster fills, until my time to join them.

The wind has subsided, allowing the rain to resume its vertical fall. It's a good sign and I start to stir. At my feet lie two cigarette butts, normally an hour's worth of smokes. I glance at my watch for confirmation. Off by ten—seventy minutes has passed. It means I'm cutting back, delaying my admission to the gathering. In a way, it comforts me to know that at the end I'll be here and nowhere else. Still, I smile at the brief postponement; the Surgeon General would be pleased.

I scan the lawn and pinpoint the spot; Uncle Kikoy's there. I'll visit him first as I always do, a pattern dictated by order of arrival.

At the gravesite, I hastily cross myself and wonder if I did it right. Is it right to left, or the reverse? It's been so long. Just to be safe, I do one of each then mumble a greeting, tell him I miss him and hope all goes well. This morning, I have a pot of poinsettias and I place it on the headstone, a small, bare marble plaque. For a year or so after he passed, his girlfriend used to leave flowers, but not a petal since. I can't blame her; she's young, younger than I am, and her life goes on. Her time with him was brief; mine went from childhood to middle age. I've assumed the task.

Dad's next, and for him I bring no flowers. Unlike my uncle Kikoy, who died an anonymous death, my father was a man of his Community; he is mourned and remembered. Flowers from me would be redundant. I slowly approach his gravesite and, just as in life, I'm not sure what to say; I'm still searching for a prayer.

I didn't talk much to Uncle Kikoy either, but that was never a problem. He barely spoke English, he was an uncle—I had lower expectations. But with Dad I had the impression, dashed by age ten, that fathers and sons were supposed to talk, to hold long heart-to-heart marathons like Ward and Beaver. It just wasn't his way to talk much to me, other than to warn or scold. What secrets did he own? What fears or hopes? What dreams had he dreamed in a different language? I never knew; he never told me.

Still I didn't mind, because he could have left us—my mother and me, my brother and sister. It would have been easy. From rumors and from examined shards of family history, I know that he'd already left one woman and her kids (his, too). But the complaints they may have are theirs, not mine. For the survivors (my shadow brothers and sisters), let them come here to howl or to curse him, or to piss on his grave. I won't, because even at our poorest, when he drove country roads looking for work, he stayed because he loved us, and I knew it.

Childhood poverty strengthens memory, and my strongest images are of Dad covered with dust and, later, with grease and scabs, blistered and discolored—the signs of accidents, burns from his welder's torch (blood money, he called it). Often I wouldn't see him for days (overtime, he said), maybe a glimpse in the morning or late at night. He did this, I knew, so his kids could avoid a life of blood money.

Over the years I grew closer to him in an odd, indirect way, through intermediaries like my mother, who told me he had stopped smoking the year I was born. Somehow, because of me, he'd quit cold a twenty-year addiction; Salem Menthols were his last brand. Later, she said, he'd carried clippings of the box scores of whatever sport I played; he'd go to Chinatown and show them to his friends. "My boy," he'd say. Sometimes, he'd show them to strangers. Still another source claimed Dad had cried at my wedding, the first one. We're even; I cried at his funeral.

I am now at his gravesite, and not even the rain, again horizontal, can turn me away. Since the funeral, I've been here two other times; this is the third. During both of those visits I searched for words—eloquent, affectionate, beautiful—that my father had never heard from me. Those words weren't there, at least I couldn't find them. Do they even exist? Dreams. A different language. I try again, then suddenly stop. It isn't necessary. Our bond was wordless; belated eloquence won't change that. A chat with the living, it's the same with the dead.

I smile. I've found my prayer.

"Got in last night," I say softly. "Tired as hell, but I'm glad I'm here." I pause. "Real glad."

Acknowledgments

The author wishes to acknowledge with appreciation the following publications in which earlier versions of some of the stories in this collection have appeared: "A Manong's Heart," in *Turning Shadows into Light*, Mayumi Tsutakawa, Alan C. Lau, editors (Seattle: Young Pine Press, 1982; "A Life Well Lived," in *The International Examiner* (1982); "Rico," in *The Seattle Review* 14:2(1992), also in *Charlie Chan Is Dead: An Anthology of Contemporary Asian-American Fiction*, Jessica Hagedorn, editor (New York: Viking/Penguin, 1993); "Home," in *The International Examiner* (1992), also in *Flippin': Filipinos on America*, Luis H. Francia, Eric Gamalinda, editors (New Brunswick, NJ: Rutgers University Press, 1996); "Dark Blue Suit" (formerly, "First, There Were the Men . . . "), in *Amerasia Journal* 19:3 (1993); "The Wedding," in *Zyzzyva* (1993); "A Matter of Faith," in *American Eyes: New Asian-American Short Stories*, Lori M. Carlson, editor (New York: Henry Holt, 1994); "August 1968," in *ReViewing Asian America: Locating Diversity*, Wendy L. Ng, Soo-Young Chin, James S. May, Gary Y. Okihiro, editors (Pullman: Washington State University Press, 1995); "A Family Gathering," in *Faultline: A Journal of Art and Literature* 4 (Fall 1995); "The Second Room," in *Under Western Eyes: Personal Essays from Asian America*, Garrett Hongo, editor (New York: Anchor/Doubleday, 1995).

Also by Peter Bacho

Cebu

"*Cebu* is a darkly comic and often painfully graphic story of the moral and cultural dilemmas that face second generation Filipino Americans in today's urban environments. Bacho is at his best in portraying the multifaceted personae of the often larger-than-life cultural types of the community. This is an exceptional book, and Peter Bacho deserves to be recognized as a major voice in contemporary literature."—*MultiCultural Review*

"This novel takes a profoundly unsettling look at a cycle of violence, revenge, and martyrdom that starts in Cebu City during the Japanese Occupation and moves to the immigrant-rich streets of present-day south Seattle. . . . a wild and provocative ride through a deeply disturbing world."—*Booklist*

Photo by Janet Alvarado. Location courtesy of Asian Boxing Arts, Seattle, Washington.

Peter Bacho is the author of the novel *Cebu*, winner of the American Book Award of the Before Columbus Foundation. He has worked as a lawyer, journalist, and teacher in California and Washington; he currently teaches in the Liberal Studies Program, University of Washington, Tacoma.